OTHER HAY HOUSE
TITLES OF RELATED INTEREST

BOOKS
Adventures of a Psychic, by Sylvia Browne
Chakra Clearing, by Doreen Virtue, Ph.D.
Conversations with the Other Side, by Sylvia Browne
Crossing Over, by John Edward
Diary of a Psychic, by Sonia Choquette
Contacting your Spirit Guide, Sylvia Browne
(Book & CD)

CARD DECKS
Dream Cards, by Leon Nacson
Healing with the Angels Oracle Cards,
by Doreen Virtue, Ph.D.
Heart and Soul, by Sylvia Browne
Messages from your Angels Oracle Cards,
by Doreen Virtue, Ph.D.
Miracle Cards, by Marianne Williamson

All of the above are available at your local bookshop,
or may be ordered through Hay House.

THE REMARKABLE STORY OF A SEVENTH SON OF A SEVENTH SON

Gordon Smith

With a foreword by
Professor Archie E. Roy
Emeritus Professor of Astronomy
at Glasgow University

Hay House, Inc.
United Kingdom • Sydney, Australia
Canada • Hong Kong • Carlsbad, California, USA

Published in the United Kingdom by:
Hay House UK Ltd, Unit B, 292 Kensal Road, London W10 5BE
Phone: +44 (0)20 8962 1230; Fax: +44 (0)20 8962 1239
www.hayhouse.co.uk

Published and distributed in Australia by:
Hay House Australia, Ltd, 18/36 Ralph St., Alexandria NSW 2015
Phone: 612-9669-4299; Fax: 612-9669-4144
www.hayhouse.com.au

Published and distributed in the United States by:
Hay House, Inc., PO Box 5100, Carlsbad, CA 92018-5100
Phone: (760) 431-7695 or (800) 654-5126; Fax: (760) 431 6948 or (800)
650-5115
www.hayhouse.com; e-mail: info@hayhouse.com

Distributed in Canada by:
Raincoast, 9050 Shaughnessy St., Vancouver, BC V6P 6E5
Phone: (604) 323-7100; Fax: (604) 323-2600

Cover Design: Steve Williams
Interior Design: e-Digital

Part of this text was previously published as Inner Visions by Pembridge
Publishing, 2000, ISBN 0 9534816 1 1

ISBN-10 1-4019-0393-2
ISBN-13 978-1-4019-0393-0
1st printing, June 2003
Reprinted 2004, 2005, 2006

Printed in Europe and Australia

*This book is dedicated to
two of my greatest teachers in life,
Jean Primrose and Albert Best,
both of whom gave selflessly
in order to help others.*

Contents

Preface

To all who read this book:

What I do means such a lot to me and for this reason I have tried to put it across as honestly as possible. People who seek my help do so because they hope to make contact with a loved one who has passed on to the spirit world. Normally, they come to me when their heart is breaking or when they have exhausted every other avenue open to them. I truly hope that this book may bring comfort and reassurance that there is life after death, not only for those who have passed away, but also for the grieving hearts left behind.

If ever I receive praise for my efforts, I often reply, 'I am not so important, but what the spirit world allows me to do for others is.'

Best wishes

Gordon Smith

FOREWORD

As a psychical researcher, it has been my good fortune over the years to have known many mediums. Some I have not only watched demonstrating on Spiritualist platforms, but also had sittings with. Others I have worked with in PRISM (Psychical Research Involving Selected Mediums), the organization set up to bring mediums and psychical researchers together in order to study and evaluate mediumistic phenomena. Some, I am happy to say, I regard as good friends of mine.

Gordon Smith is one of those friends, which is one of the reasons I was delighted to be asked to write a foreword. *Spirit Messenger* was an enjoyable book to read. It made me laugh out loud in places where Gordon's sense of modesty and self-deprecating humour push him into deflating any budding feelings that he is in any way special.

But he *is* special. Gordon Smith is a medium, a person who, in every other way, leads a normal life, working as a hairdresser, yet who demonstrates again and again his ability to receive information he simply could not have obtained through the use of the five senses. This is precise, detailed information, startlingly relevant to the recipient, conveyed either at a meeting-place or during a private sitting.

Apart from Spiritualists and psychical researchers, the public knows little about mediums. In films, TV and books, people are invariably presented with grossly distorted caricatures of mediums. In Noel Coward's *Blithe Spirit*, Madame Arcati is a figure of fun, although, in due course, Charles, the sceptical husband, is shocked to find that she is genuine after all.

The sceptic, especially if they have never studied mediums, easily explains it all away. Any ostensible physical phenomena are due, they say, to sleight of hand, misdirection of attention or the practised use of ingeniously fabricated or carefully concealed apparatus. As for the mental medium, they say they produce their effects by a mixture of swift adjustment of a generalized statement, cold reading and careful attention to the body language and verbal responses given by the eager-to-be-convinced recipient.

I have no doubt that in many places throughout the world there exist fake psychics or people who have genuinely misled themselves into believing they have psychic ability. Many of the former are tricksters of a particularly nasty kind, greedily leeching money from people who have lost loved ones, people anxious to be convinced that death is not the end and that they can find evidence their loved ones still exist. Such frauds deserve exposure not only because they prey on an extremely vulnerable section of the community but also because of the bad name they give to genuine mediums.

Where I and the sceptic who dismisses all ostensible paranormal abilities part company is that over the years I have become convinced by the sheer weight of evidence that genuine mediums exist. Some I have met and studied; others I regret never having known. I had the privilege, for example, of knowing for many years the Glasgow medium Albert Best. There is no way the accurate information he gave a friend of mine and me could have been obtained in any normal manner.

Among the mediums who were before my time were Mrs Piper, Mrs Leonard, Mrs Willett, Geraldine Cummins and Eileen Garrett, to name but a few. Over the decades, some of the most intelligent, cautious, initially sceptical psychical researchers studied them; people of the calibre of Dr Richard Hodgson, Professor William James, Sir Oliver Lodge, Professor Charles Richet and Gerald, Second Earl of Balfour. What they found transformed their open-minded scepticism into a firm belief in the ability of at least some people's minds to operate outside time and space. Some, like Hodgson and Lodge, went further: they finally became convinced that the best explanation was that we survive the bodily change we call death and, under certain circumstances, can communicate with those left behind.

Most Spiritualists and most mediums believe that a medium – as the name implies – acts as an intermediary between those who have gone on, having left their dead bodies, and those still in this world. They believe that the medium demonstrating from a public platform in a church or hall, or giving a sitting to someone, is conveying information from Spirit to the relevant person to provide evidence that the loved one has survived. In hundreds of Spiritualist churches, mediums demonstrate throughout the UK and in other countries, and have been doing so for over 150 years.

There is, of course, a wide spectrum of mediumistic ability, from marvellous to mediocre. It would appear that, as with almost any other human activity, there are superstars, stars and barely luminous glow-worms! Sometimes, as has been known for more than a century, the entire range of brightness can be shown by the same medium at different times.

Not only can mediums have their off days, but they can also be affected by the sitter from hell who sits back stubbornly, arms folded, with a defiant look of utter disbelief on their face, plainly thinking, 'Go on, astonish me!' Yet sometimes they are astonished when mediums of the calibre of Albert Best or Gordon Smith provide exact names, addresses, events and descriptions sharply relevant to their life and the lives of those they have known.

I am not a Spiritualist but a psychical researcher who, by the very nature of my scientific training, deals in probabilities. But what makes a medium? Are they born, do they develop or suddenly become mediums at some stage of their lives? Is it like football, where it seems reasonable to suppose that superstars like George Best (a nephew of Albert Best) and Stanley Matthews are born naturally gifted in the quickness of their physical reactions and subsequently, by long training and experience, perfect their abilities, honing the sharpness of their astonishing talent?

Many of the great mediums have shown signs of psychic ability from childhood. Such a child is fortunate to have parents who are familiar with these matters. More often in our western society, parents react in a confused, dismayed or even angry fashion, telling the child to stop fantasizing and forbidding them to tell such 'lies'. Sometimes, however, the child's developing sensitivity is recognized by another medium so that help is given to come to terms with it or to develop the talent further.

The path leading to a career as a medium is by no means an easy one to follow. Often it has no signposts and the developing medium's life is frequently full of doubts and difficulties. Nevertheless, when one compares the accounts given by mediums, it is difficult to avoid the conclusion that among their diverse upbringings and experiences there is a common theme. They are all aware of other facets of reality; they sense beyond the five senses; they are in touch with ... what? By continuing to study mediums patiently, carefully and comparatively, we have a chance to find out, a means of exploring the deepest mysteries of human personality and spirituality.

I welcome this enjoyable and informative book, and thank Gordon for giving us this insight into the development of his own mediumship. Read it and journey with someone who has found himself a voyager on uncharted seas.

Professor Archie E. Roy
Emeritus Professor of Astronomy at Glasgow
University

ACKNOWLEDGEMENTS

I wish to express my grateful thanks to Linda Rowan, for encouragement in getting started, Tony Ortzen, for his editing skills, and Kathy Sorley, for assisting on the original manuscript.

I also wish to thank Tricia Robertson, Dronma, Stella Blair, Rosalind Cattanach, Richard Rosin, Lee Bright, Christine Peebles, Mary Armour, Jim McManus, Martin Boyce and Mrs Preston, without whose contributions and assistance I could not have written this book.

Last – but certainly not least – love and thanks to my sons Paul and Steven for putting up with me!

CHAPTER ONE

It was Wednesday 9 March 1987. It must have been just before 6.30 a.m. that I began to wake up. Somewhere between sleep and waking, a vision of a young man began to build up in front of me. I thought I was dreaming, but this dream was becoming more and more vivid. The young man was now fully visible. I recognized him as the brother of my workmate and close friend Christine Peebles.

Christine and I had known each other since childhood. We were brought up in the same area, went to the same schools and eventually worked together in a hairdressing salon in Glasgow. Christine and her brother Brian had just bought a flat together in the West End of Glasgow. Both of them seemed very happy with their new home. In fact, Christine appeared more content and positive about her future than she had in months. Still, a disturbing feeling ran through my body that morning. I knew something was very wrong.

I sat up in bed abruptly, and with that, the vision of Brian disappeared. He seemed to dissolve through the bedroom floor, yet still my heart began to race, even though there hadn't been anything disturbing about Brian's appearance. He had just seemed to be standing in front of me wearing blue jeans and a red checked shirt. He had been smiling and had appeared very reassuring, but this terrible feeling of alarm stayed with me. And I couldn't decide whether I was dreaming or whether I really had seen someone standing there.

Just then I had the urge to switch on the radio by my bedside. The clock was showing 6.30 a.m. I flicked the radio switch and heard a man's voice booming out the local news: 'A fire has swept through a West End flat in Glasgow...'

Suddenly my heart was almost bursting out of my chest whilst my ears were ringing very loudly. In my mind's eye, I caught a vision of two policemen standing in front of me and heard myself saying, 'It must be Christine.' I just *knew* it must be her flat that had been burned out. I feared that she was dead.

I never caught the end of the news. There was a loud knock on my front door. I jumped out of bed, threw on some clothes and, still half-dressed, opened the door to find two policemen standing in front of me. Shock swept through me like a bolt of lightning. My eyes must have been as wide as saucers. It was all I could do just to stare at them.

'Gordon Smith?' asked one of the constables.

'Yes,' I replied.

'There's been an accident,' he continued. 'I have been asked to pass these keys on to you from a Miss Christine Peebles.'

'Is she alright?' I asked.

'She is with a friend now,' said the policeman. 'I am afraid that is all I can say at the moment.'

I took the keys and closed the door. They were for the hairdresser's salon, which Christine was due to open as it was my day off. It suddenly dawned on me that she must be safe, that she wasn't dead after all. *Oh dear!* I thought. *It must be Brian. Poor Christine.* Still, the policeman hadn't said that anyone had died in the accident. Maybe I had imagined it all.

But it wasn't just my imagination. By the time I reached the salon just before 9 a.m., the news had come through that Brian had been killed in a tragic fire and that his sister and a friend had been saved.

The strange experience that woke me kept playing over in my mind the whole day. I could still see Brian's face smiling happily at me and wondered why I had had the vision of two policemen standing at my door just minutes before they arrived.

Amid the sadness I was feeling for my friend, my mind began to replay all sorts of memories of my childhood, memories I had locked away in the deepest vaults of my consciousness. A floodgate opened in my mind. It seemed that Brian's passing had disturbed a latent psychic ability in me, one I had not experienced since my teenage years.

I was then 25 years of age. My life had taken a different direction since my psychic childhood and my attention had turned towards my career in hairdressing, which I had started at the age of eighteen. During this time I had married and had two sons who, together with my work, took up most of my waking time. Looking back, I don't think that there had been much time to allow my mind to drift to thoughts of the psychic world that had so often been part of my early life.

After the funeral service, I asked Christine if there was anything I could do for her. She asked if I would take her to a Spiritualist church to see a medium, so she might hear some news of Brian on the Other Side. I felt it would be wrong for her to attend something like this so soon after her brother's death, but she was so insistent that I could hardly refuse. I made some enquiries and found out that there was going to be a very good medium taking a service at the Glasgow Association of Spiritualists in Somerset Place. So it was that Christine and I, together with Brian's fiancée Fiona, attended the meeting.

I had never been in a Spiritualist church in my life and I had no idea what to expect. I must admit, I assumed that we would be sitting round a table while some elderly lady closed her eyes and asked the air around her if there was anybody there.

The three of us sat together in the front row of the church and the medium was brought onto the platform. She was Mary Duffy of Edinburgh, a woman in her sixties, I would have said, with a very kind face. She seemed educated, spoke with a very polite Edinburgh accent and didn't fit the image we had conjured up of how a medium should look.

The meeting began with hymn-singing and prayers, like any ordinary church service, and it was all very pleasant. Then the medium gave a talk on Spiritualism and began her demonstration of clair-voyance. Almost immediately she turned to our small party in the front row and addressed Christine and Fiona with great sympathy: 'I would not have to be a medium to know that you have just suffered a great loss.' Both Christine and Fiona began to sob.

Mary was very reassuring and managed to relay a message from Christine's mother, who had passed on several years earlier. She continued by saying that Christine should try to seek out a medium called Albert Best when she felt that the time was right, for she believed he would be the one person who could help her through her grief.

She then turned to me and said, 'Young man, I have never given a message like this from a public platform before, but I must tell you that your grand-mother in the spirit world is telling me that you will one day stand on this very platform and give spirit communication to people as I am doing now.'

As she said these words to me, a very bright light seemed to be emanating from her body, becoming brighter with every word she spoke. She urged me to find a good development circle and to be patient and allow the spirit world to develop my gift of clairvoyance. Then she went on to her next contact.

When the service was over, the three of us discussed the evening's events and agreed that it all seemed positive. Christine was very eager to contact this man Albert Best. Unbelievable as it may seem, she didn't get that sitting with him until almost nine years later, but the results were quite amazing, as she received a communication from Brian that was better than she could have imagined.

I, on the other hand, was about to take my first step on a spiritual journey that would change my life completely.

CHAPTER TWO

I suppose it was inevitable that I would encounter Spiritualism at some point, for looking back over my childhood there were so many occasions when I saw people from the spirit world or heard voices no one else was aware of.

The first time I remember such an incident I was about seven or eight and had just come through a bad bout of rheumatic fever. After leaving hospital, I had to spend some time at home to build up my strength. It was during this period that I had my first clear spirit vision.

I was playing in our front garden at home on my own, as my brothers and friends had gone back to school after the lunch break. As I remember it, I walked out into the street. It was a bright, sunny day. Our road seemed to be deserted until, from the end, I could see a man walking toward me. As he approached me, I smiled. It was Ummy, a friend of my parents.

No one in my family can remember how he got that nickname, but his visits were always greatly welcomed, especially by us children. All the youngsters in our street knew him. He used to give us an old penny or a threepenny bit, depending on how he had fared at the racetrack. Ummy spent most of his time around the racetracks of Scotland. He was a tic-tac man and worked for nearly all the bookies at one time or other. He always visited us after having a good day at the races and we all used to mob him when he came off the number four bus that ran through our street. He was the kind of man that youngsters loved. He would sing and tell us corny jokes, although now I suspect he would have a few drinks before arriving! Nevertheless, he was a harmless man and very kind. He belonged to an older generation which saw nothing untoward about giving pennies to children in the street and he always seemed to have time to play with us before going indoors to see my parents.

On this particular day, he was walking toward me from the far end of our street, singing something about Dalbeth. I did not know what this meant, but joined in with him, singing, 'We will be buried in Dalbeth.'

As he got closer to me, Ummy smiled and just stood looking at me. I have never forgotten the expression of joy on his face. He looked so bright and happy.

Then, as I went to go forward to him, something stopped me in my tracks. My feet were rooted to the ground. Ummy started to move backwards, waving at me as he went. I remember wanting to go with him, but I couldn't move forward. Just before he disappeared out of sight, I heard him say goodbye.

As soon as he was gone, I ran indoors to tell my mother. She was standing at the kitchen sink; I think she was peeling potatoes or something. I was very excited. I grabbed her skirt and impatiently blurted out what had just occurred. As she looked at me, her eyes were wide with disbelief. To my astonishment, she shouted at me to stop telling lies.

'You couldn't have seen him!' she said. 'It's all in your mind.' There was almost a look of fear on her face.

I couldn't understand it. Why she would say this to me? It wasn't until some time later I learned that Ummy had died about a week or so earlier and that he had been buried in Dalbeth Cemetery in the East End of Glasgow. My family had considered me too young to be told.

After that experience I became rather reluctant to tell adults about my encounters with spirit people. Nevertheless, on that particular occasion I had no idea that I was talking to a spirit person, as Ummy had looked so solid, so real, to me.

As a young boy, I had also many precognitive experiences and visions of the future. Mostly, these spontaneous predictions came when I was daydreaming or playing with toys. One Sunday afternoon while I was playing with some toy cars, my mother and father came in and didn't notice me behind the couch. They happened to be talking about Joan, one of my elder sisters, who had gone out for the day with her then boyfriend. He had borrowed a car to take her for a drive.

I remember standing up from behind the couch where I had been kneeling and interrupting my parents' conversation to tell them that my sister was in a police station in Carlisle – many miles from Glasgow – and would be home tomorrow. They both looked at me. Then they went back to their conversation. My sister had not been out long, so there was no way she could have been anywhere near Carlisle. Apart from that, she and her boyfriend were supposed to be driving locally, so it must have sounded as though this over-imaginative child was at it again.

However, later that evening, after I had had a bath ready for school the next morning, I was sitting with the rest of the family in the living-room when my father mentioned he was concerned about Joan, as it had been some time since she had gone out. My mother made light of it and said she thought they would be back soon. Not long after that I was put to bed.

The following morning when I got up for school nothing appeared to be wrong. What I didn't know was that some time during the night my parents had received a call from the police saying that Joan and her boyfriend were safe – and that they would be spending the night in the police station in Carlisle. They hadn't done anything wrong, but the car they were driving had broken down somewhere in the Borders and they couldn't get it repaired until the following day.

By the time I came home for lunch, my sister had returned safely. Nothing was said about my prediction, but when I walked into the living-room, everyone went quiet and just looked at me. For a moment I felt strange, then I just asked for my lunch and went about my day like any normal ten-year-old boy.

Many people say that mediums cannot or should not predict the future; I would say that whether or not mediums or psychics should do so is a matter of circumstance. I am sure that sometimes the spirit world feels it is right to give the outcome of a particular situation if this is helpful to the recipient in time of need. Bear in mind that there are many occasions when it is *not* needful to know the outcome of certain events in our lives and to do so might even be disturbing. A medium will learn to trust their spirit inspirers in these matters.

As for me, I don't know how many times in

my young life my mother would shout at me, 'Would you stop staring up at that ceiling! You have a really stupid look on your face when you do that. Now go out and play with the rest of the kids!' Sometimes she would ask, 'What is it that you keep looking up at?' I never used to answer, just get up and go outside. I couldn't tell her that I could see lights dancing around our ceiling or that Sarah was talking to me in my head.

Sarah Reilly Davis was my grandmother on my mother's side. She died in 1945 at the young age of 42, the same night that my mother and father were married. This left my mother, aged 19, to bring up her younger brothers and sisters. Then, just after their wedding, my father was drafted overseas as part of his Royal Navy service. This meant that my mother was left bringing up children without her new husband while carrying the grief of having just lost her mother. How hard that must have been, especially in those days when there wasn't much of anything to go around. Now, whenever I feel that life is getting me down, I try to remind myself how hard my parents' lives have been and I am uplifted when I think of how they came through so many difficult situations.

It certainly makes me feel humble and proud to have parents as strong as Sam and Liz. Between them, they have helped so many people. They are both typical Glaswegians who feel much better about giving to others than taking for themselves.

Many people have cause to thank them for their generosity, including me, the youngest of their children.

My mother says that when I was born, the midwife who delivered me said that being the seventh son of a seventh son – the same as my father – meant I was going to be very spiritually gifted. Yet here I was being told off for looking at spirit lights or hearing my grandmother's voice in my head. It was said that Sarah was very psychic and used to read cups for people. If that were true, then why wouldn't she come back and talk to her psychic grandson?

When I was 11 years old, my parents took me to visit an old friend of theirs, Ella, who lived in Blairgowrie, Perthshire. It was during this trip that I had my first meeting with a Spiritualist medium.

We were there for the weekend and on the second day Ella's sister Sadie arrived. She was a small, stout lady, probably in her mid-sixties. She had short grey hair and dark brown eyes. After some small talk between my parents and the two ladies, Ella asked me, in her strong Perthshire accent, to sit in the kitchen, just off the living-room. She gave me some paper and coloured pens, told me I should draw for a while and said she would come and fetch me in a short time.

I couldn't settle. There seemed to be some-thing going on and I wanted to be in on it. I suppose, like most children, I didn't like being left out. I was curious to know what was happening in the next room.

Finally, after what felt like an eternity to me, I was allowed to rejoin my parents and the two ladies. I could feel an excitement between the adults. My mother was saying she had witnessed something quite amazing, whilst my father had a look of bewilderment on his face, although he remained quiet. I didn't say anything, but was dying to know what had gone on. It wasn't long before I found out.

Sadie asked my mother if she could try some healing with me. I had no idea what this meant or what she expected me to do. My mother agreed and I was asked to sit on a chair in front of Sadie. She told me to close my eyes and then put her hands on my shoulders.

Within a short period of time, I felt a slight vibration, as though the chair I was sitting on was revolving. In my mind I saw faces of people – men and women. Some looked as though they came from long ago and others from a more recent time. Only one of these faces was familiar to me and no one spoke or gave me messages to pass on. Then the healer called to her sister, saying, 'Ella, come quickly! Feel this energy!' She sounded very excited. I wanted to open my eyes at this point, but couldn't. Sadie repeated the same word over and over again: 'clairvoyance'. Ella agreed that there was indeed a very strong feeling of clairvoyance around the boy.

I was still sensing the vibration – in fact, it became even more intense. Then I felt a sudden urge to laugh. Though I tried to hold it back, in my mind's eye I had a picture of both these well-built women gyrating all around me and the urge was just getting stronger.

Though my eyes were still tightly shut, I could hear everything going on around me. I was aware of my mother's presence – and knew she wasn't pleased with me! She was whispering to my father, who is partially deaf, something about me making a fool of these two ladies.

'Look at him,' she said. 'I'll kill him when I get him home!'

My father, attempting to make out what she was saying, replied in an even louder whisper, 'What is it you're trying to say, Lizzie? I can't hear you.'

'Keep your voice down, you silly little man!' she said. 'Your son is laughing under his breath at Sadie.' She then turned to Ella and said, 'He has always been a very nervous child.' At this point, I burst out laughing.

After my laughter subsided, Sadie spoke to me quietly and asked what I had seen when my eyes were first closed. I gave a description of the lady I knew was Sarah, my grandmother, even though I had never seen a picture of her in my life. In fact, I did not see a photograph of her until ten years after this. Then I gave descriptions of other people I had seen. When I had finished, Sadie said, 'You have no idea how gifted this child is.'

I looked at my mother, who did not seem amused. 'Is that right?' she asked. She thought I had made the whole thing up just to please Sadie.

Sadie continued by saying, 'By the time he reaches his late twenties, he will become a clairvoyant, after which he will travel the world and be known as one of the most famous mediums of his time. He will also heal people in his life.'

My mother interrupted this great spiel by saying, 'Sammy, would you listen to that, eh? Our Gordon's going to be famous in some way!'

My father, who has always been a quiet and very patient man, replied, 'Aye, Lizzie, that's good, eh.'

After this great proclamation had finished and things had settled down again, I overheard my parents talking about what had occurred before I had entered the room. Apparently Sadie had spoken to the spirit of my father's dead father and had given a perfect description of how he would have looked. She had then predicted that my father, who wasn't working at this time because he had developed rheumatoid arthritis in his joints, would restart his job at a certain time later in the year. She had given him healing and although she may not have cured his condition, the pain did ease off enough to enable him to continue working at the same firm until his retirement some 20 years later. She also gave many other pieces of evidence of life after death as well as predictions that all came true.

I was so excited that I was going to be famous as a great something-or-other, even though I had already forgotten the word 'clairvoyant', that I couldn't wait to get home to tell everyone. Here was this lady telling me that it was alright to hear voices! I was filled with joy, probably because it seemed I had been picked out and told I was going to be good at something. I started to try and imagine travelling around the world in the way Sadie had forecast.

The next day, as we travelled back to Glasgow by train, I asked my mother, 'What was that word Sadie said I was going to be?'

'Listen, you,' she said, 'you can just forget all that nonsense, d'you hear? I don't want you to let that go to your head.'

'But Mum…' I protested.

'I don't want to hear another word about it!'

And that was me dismissed. My great fame was never to be mentioned again.

It seems strange to me now that so many of these childhood memories were buried deep inside me for such a long time. But at the time I was often afraid to tell people about my psychic experiences since I was always scolded for 'telling lies' or told it was all in my imagination. I was even told it was bad to have such experiences. It's no wonder I wanted to stop hearing and seeing spirit people. However, now I can see that the people around me were only trying to protect me from something they simply did not understand.

CHAPTER THREE

A month or so after the death of Brian Peebles, I
began to visit all the Spiritualist churches I could
find. Although every medium I encountered told
me I should join a 'development circle' to develop
my gifts, no one ever explained how I might do
this. Many circles are held in mediums' homes,
with entry by invitation only.

After much searching, I found a group at the
small Spiritualist church in Glasgow's West Princes
Street. It was run by Jean Primrose, a lady in her late
seventies, who had devoted most of her life to
Spiritualism and headed this church for almost 50
years. As well as being President of the church,
Jean was also a very gifted medium and healer. She
called a spade a spade, never suffering fools gladly.
Hers was what is known as an 'open circle', with
people coming and going from time to time, so I

was welcomed into the Thursday night group.

This became my spiritual classroom for the next eight years. During this time, I learned to develop the spiritual gift that had been with me since childhood. Not only was I taught to develop mediumship, but I was also encouraged to cultivate the healing gift that had been predicted so many years before.

However, spiritual development is not only about healing or clairvoyance. In addition, it opens up your mind and fosters self-awareness, which allows you to gain a greater understanding of your spiritual nature, of other people and indeed of life itself.

The first night I sat in the circle I was very apprehensive, as I had no idea what would happen. I remember thinking I would like to get up and leave, but then Mrs Primrose walked in. She was no more than four feet ten inches tall, but her presence seemed to fill the whole room. Everyone sat up straight, like schoolchildren at the sudden appearance of their headmistress.

The room was about the size of a large sitting-room, which at one time it would have been. It was part of an old Georgian house which in recent years had been let out as three separate properties: the church rooms on the ground floor and two flats above. The room we occupied was to the front of the property, the largest of four that together made up the church. The others were an office, a small library and a kitchen/tearoom, where people congregated after each service.

Here I was at my first circle, sitting in a group of about 40 people, with chairs set around the walls. It was more of a square than a circle. Still, it seemed to serve the purpose. I sat near the front, not too far from where Mrs Primrose was conducting proceedings. Just behind me was a small wooden rostrum with a glass front on which sat a statue of praying hands. Hanging on the wall behind this was a large lithograph of Christ, which I found very calming.

Mrs Primrose asked everyone to put their feet flat on the floor and sit comfortably, then began to sing 'The Lord is my Shepherd'. Soon everyone joined in. For the first time, I had a strong feeling of harmony as the voices blended together. The hymn was followed by the Lord's Prayer and another hymn, and then the circle commenced.

'Close your eyes, relax and listen to the music,' Mrs Primrose instructed. I was anxious to know if there were any spirits floating around the room. In the midst of my mental wanderings, the silence was broken by a man's voice, speaking in what sounded like an Indian accent. He said he was a teacher from a very high realm of the spirit world and that he had come to teach us about compassion.

I couldn't keep my eyes closed any longer and hoped that this evolved entity might be visible to the naked eye. But when I looked toward the far end of the church, all I could see was a short, stout, grey-haired man in his fifties, on his feet, eyes tightly shut, speaking in what now sounded like a very exaggerated Asian accent.

At first, I did try to make sense of his so-called 'philosophy', but not too long into the supposedly spiritual dialogue, I noticed that the highly evolved one's Asian accent became padded with Glaswegian dialect, with phrases like 'We have come to help you, so we huv' or 'Try tae look efter yur weans better this yies ur dae'in' and so on. (The latter translates as something like 'Try to look after your children better than you are at the moment.')

As if this wasn't bad enough, the Glasgow guru was then joined by a huge woman sitting opposite him purporting to channel an Oriental woman. She began her spiritual address with the words 'By the way' in what sounded like Chinese-restaurant English. I was on the point of laughing out aloud when thankfully Mrs Primrose interrupted this crazy charade by asking both parties to sit down and be quiet. *Sanity at long last*, I thought.

There are times when people's imaginations can run wild, especially in this type of situation, and it would appear that Mrs Primrose did not take this obvious playacting too seriously. I also noticed that May, Mrs Primrose's daughter, was very attuned to who was genuine and who was not, although I am sure the two individuals mentioned were not deliberately fraudulent, just misguided or suffering from wishful thinking.

Apart from these dramatic outbursts of Glaswegian philosophy, the rest of the evening went quite well. I didn't experience any encounters with the spirit world that first night, although several people did. These were people who had sat quietly and continued their meditation while the Asian floorshow was taking place. It appeared to me that the thing to do in a development circle was to sit still, clear your mind, allow your senses to heighten and wait for the spirit world to draw close to you and 'impress' you with the messages they wished to convey.

After the circle was brought to a close, most of the people gathered in the small tearoom, where they shared their experiences of the night. I listened intently, intrigued by some of the stories. I think I failed to recognize the finer points of the circle the first night, but I realized that if I was going to try to develop my spirituality, I would have to learn the rights and wrongs of Spiritualist circles. If I was to continue in this class, I would have to recognize the difference between my own imaginings and my natural ability to perceive spirit people.

Spiritual development is above all a learning experience and in every training programme in our lives, we will make mistakes. We learn from these mistakes. But if we can laugh at them too, it makes learning so much easier. There's no such thing as right and wrong if you are willing to learn from a situation. Many of my greatest learning experiences have come about through witnessing how *not* to do things. Let me highlight some of the more light-hearted moments on my learning journey in the development circle.

A lady who sat in our circle for only one session confidently claimed this was enough time to become a medium of great importance. She must have considered herself a bit like a Kodak film – if she were left for an hour or so in a darkened room, then she would indeed develop!

Never a night passed in our circle without someone claiming to have some notable spirit guide or other. In my time, there were a couple of John the Baptists, quite a number of Saint Teresas, the odd Gandhi here and there and too many popes and bishops to count. Oh, and even Jesus was purported to be channelling through one man openly and a few more on the quiet. Wouldn't you think that these people had done their bit for spirituality when they were on Earth?

I will always remember the remark made by one of the women in the circle after a man in a so-called 'trance' claimed that John the Baptist was speaking through him. When her friend asked if she would like to be baptized by the so-called 'holy one', she replied: 'I think I will wait until he channels someone else. That big idiot he's channelling through now gives me the willies.' Apparently, this same man claimed to have the Blessed Virgin in his cupboard at home. No wonder the success rate of healing at Lourdes has plummeted – Mary is in a pantry in Glasgow!

If there is a problem with spirit guides, it is the way people interpret them. Some people get caught up with the idea of having important spirit guides. Sadly, this is the image many people have of all mediums and Spiritualists. I do wish people would think for a moment before believing such nonsense. A little bit of common sense is all that is required.

During one of the monthly discussion groups that were held after our development circle, the man who was chairing that evening threw out a question to us, one that is often put to mediums: 'Why are spirit guides either North American Indians or ancient Chinese masters?'

Whilst most other sitters searched for a deep and meaningful answer, I said, 'Could it be there is such a long waiting list for that type of position on the Other Side that that's as far as they've got? I suppose people like us have no chance?' Somehow, I don't really believe that's the answer, though!

If nothing else, I developed a sense of humour in the development circle. The ability to laugh at some of the funny situations was what allowed me and many others to carry on with our spiritual lessons. And I am certain that those on the

Other Side love nothing more than hearing us laugh. But aside from the humour, there were also times when spirits allowed us to have some of the most beautiful experiences, moments I will always remember. Most of these tremendous events were very personal, so there is no point in sharing them with anyone else. Spiritual events seem to lose their importance when you share them with other people – they can only truly be understood by the person who experiences them.

As well as continuing my own development, I witnessed some fine mediumship during this time. In the eight years I attended this circle I can honestly say that I witnessed some phenomenal happenings, especially the trance gift of a very special teacher. One of the true qualities of any medium, no matter which field of mediumship they work in, is humility, and I consider myself fortunate to have been taught by such a medium. She was a true trance medium and whenever she allowed herself to be used as a channel, you could feel the very essence of the spirit people who spoke through her. For the purpose of this book, I shall use only her first name, Laura.

Even though I have witnessed many sessions of trance through Laura, I shall recount only one, which took place in the church after we finished our circle. As we sat in the well-lit room, it was clear that something was happening. You can always tell when spirit friends are close, for the atmosphere in the room totally changes. The temperature drops, but not in a chilly way. It is as though the heat in the room is being used to fuel events about to take place. I am never uncomfortable with this change. If anything, it is quite exciting.

On this occasion Laura seemed to drift off into trance, as she did very naturally. Some trance mediums go through great dramatic scenes, which I always think highly suspect. But any time Laura went into trance there was never any fuss or bother. We all waited to hear who would come through and speak to us that night. Usually, it would be one of Laura's guides, but this time it was a man who sounded confused and afraid, and was asking if he could be left alone.

'Who are you?' I asked.

He told me his real name, but I will call him Mr Brown.

'When did you die?' I continued.

'I'm not dead,' he replied rather indignantly.

Oh, I thought, *maybe he is calling from a nearby phone box!*

'What do you mean, you haven't died?'

'I'm here in hospital,' he said.

'Which hospital?' I asked.

Mr Brown told us the name of the hospital and also the ward number. All of this could later be checked, as it was a Glasgow hospital not too far from where we were. Mr Brown went on to tell us that his body was in a comatose state and that his wife and daughters were gathered around his bedside and were very upset. He couldn't wake up and was afraid to die because he didn't think he had always been a good person. He would much rather stay where he was, but hated to upset his family like this.

How very sad, I thought. Here was this man lying there sensing how upset his family were because of his condition, yet afraid to confront his fear of the afterlife because he believed there would be some heavy debt to pay.

Mrs Primrose spoke to the man, telling him he had nothing to fear on the Other Side and that he would be met by loved ones already there. She also told him that he must not allow his family to hang around his bedside too much longer and must consider letting go whenever he was able to.

Mr Brown seemed to pull back at this point and after a short period of time Laura regained full consciousness. She gave us an account of the experience from her point of view, explaining that she felt herself floating out of her body and following a small light drifting in front of her. The light became stronger and stronger, and at one point opened up before her like a pair of curtains. At this stage, Laura saw a man lying in a hospital bed beneath her. Three women were sitting around the bed, all very upset. Then the man lying in the bed began to float up toward her. Laura remained there for a time just observing the scene, but was then drawn back toward us.

The following day, I checked to see if there was such a man in that hospital ward. Believe it or not, there was. I wasn't able to obtain any information about his condition as I was not a family member. But what an amazing experience.

The conclusion to this story came two days later when I got a call from one of the other people who had sat with us that night asking me if I had the evening paper and if so, to look at the death notices – and there it was. Mr Brown had 'gone home'. The obituary said that he passed peacefully in a certain Glasgow hospital the previous evening … and that he would be much missed by his loving wife and devoted daughters.

Laura's mediumship has always been outstanding. The type of work that she does often seems unbelievable and yet has always proved to be correct. I must say I am glad to have been taught by one so humble and understated in her work for the Other Side. So often she has given herself to the spirit world in order that others may be helped, yet she never accepts praise or thanks. I would like to think that all practising mediums could learn from her example.

Having witnessed the rights and wrongs of spiritual development – and of course made many mistakes – I soon learned that spiritual growth comes from within. If anything, the mystery of development is not about learning, but *unlearning*. This may sound like a contradiction, but it is not. It is clear to me that when people first enter into spiritual development, they are so hungry for knowledge that they practically devour everything on the subject – every book they can read, every lecture or discussion they can attend. If ever there is a spiritual programme on television, they will be glued to it, no matter whether it's good or bad. This is what my Buddhist friend calls 'spiritual shopping'. But before long they find they have become very confused, totally sick and spiritually bloated. They have had enough.

Like most people starting on the spiritual path, I too tended to overindulge. I remember reading about six books all on spiritual and religious subjects at the same time. I was attending everything I could – clairvoyant demonstrations, discussions, healing groups. Finally, my head was dizzy with all of this, so I went to Mrs Primrose and asked for help on the matter. 'Nil by mind' was her advice. She told me to stop trying to learn things in such a hurry. It was time to allow all that I had swallowed to be digested. I did, and I must say she was correct. All of a sudden, spiritual development became fun. Because I stopped *trying* to be a medium, my natural gift began to resurface.

I have learned so much from the teachers I've been fortunate enough to know in my life, like Mrs Primrose, Laura, Albert Best and so many more.

This is not because they were teachers of great mysteries or secret knowledge, but more because of the people they were. Each of them had known much adversity and tragedy in their lives, but somehow managed to overcome all obstacles to become much stronger and display great dignity in the process.

It is now my understanding of spiritual development that lessons are laid in front of us in our everyday lives and we have to accept them with grace. A good teacher is one who does not tell you what to do, but steers you toward your lessons.

On many occasions, Mrs Primrose said to me that she knew I would make certain mistakes during my development. When I asked her why she never warned me of them, she told me, 'Son, I always wanted to, but these were lessons for you to learn. Who am I to deprive you of your experiences?'

This is how I recognize a teacher – someone who says little, but knows much.

CHAPTER FOUR

The shift from development circle to platform medium is one that I shall never forget. It reminded me of when I was training as a hairdresser at college. Whilst in college, I felt confident and eager to practise what I had learned, but when the time came to begin working in a real salon, it seemed that everything I had been taught went right out of the window! Becoming a medium was much the same in that my confidence in the circle was such that I was able to stand up in front of everyone and give spirit messages without a problem. But when asked to appear before a packed church for a Sunday service, I was a nervous wreck.

Whenever people who feel they have a clairvoyant gift ask me how to become a medium, I always answer, 'If the spirit world wants you to work for it, it will make sure you are in the right place at the right time. The chance will never go past you.' This was certainly true for me.

One Sunday night while driving to church, I became aware of an irritating feeling in my stomach. It was the same type of sensation that I got just before I had a psychic experience or premonition. Then I heard a voice in my head telling me to prepare. *Prepare for what?* I thought.

It all became clear to me when I reached the church. As I pulled up in my car, I noticed that the Vice-President and Secretary were both standing at the doorway looking quite anxious. When I approached them, Steve, the Vice-President, said, 'The medium hasn't arrived.'

'Isn't there a medium in the house?' I said, trying to make light of the situation.

'No, and what's more Mrs Primrose is at another church tonight,' he replied.

There was about a minute to go before the service was due to start and it looked as though we were not going to have a guest medium ... until Mima, the Secretary, suggested that I go on.

'Me!' I gasped, looking in amazement at the two of them.

'Well,' Mima went on, 'you always give good messages in the circle.'

After some further protesting, I finally agreed in the hope that the scheduled medium would turn up in time to save me.

Here I was, some four years or so after going

along to my first development circle, about to try to demonstrate my clairvoyant abilities in public! I can't begin to describe how nervous I was at that moment. As I walked onto the platform behind Steve and Mima, who were chairing and reading respectively, I could feel all my insides shaking like jelly.

During the introductions, hymn-singing and readings that preceded my work, I prayed. I prayed so hard that I thought my head was going to burst open. I made so many bargains with God that there was nothing left of my soul worth keeping. I even offered the ultimate bargain: 'Dear God, if You help me to get through this, I promise I will give up smoking.' I wonder how many other mediums can remember that one? Prayer – the last refuge of every doubter.

No more time for prayers, no more room for doubt, here I was being introduced as that night's medium. The last word that passed through my mind as I approached the rostrum was 'Help!' But then something very strange happened. It was as if I were a lightbulb and had just been switched on. All the nervousness and trepidation I felt disappeared the moment I went out on a limb.

Typically, I used humour to get myself started. My opening line was, 'The light has gone to you, madam,' pointing to the most serious-looking person in the room. Then I said, 'No, it hasn't really. I've just always fancied saying that ever since I read my first Doris Stokes' book.' Doris, who passed on some years ago, was one of Britain's most famous mediums and packed out the world-famous London Palladium theatre several times. Anyway, everyone laughed, including the lady, and immediately I relaxed enough to allow the spirit people to pass their messages through to their loved ones in the church.

I can't honestly say that I remember too much about the information I gave to people that first night. I was just so relieved to get it over with, even though part of me was really enjoying it. The moment I was told to finish the service, I began to shake like a leaf on an autumn day!

To my surprise, I had done quite well. People were coming up to me and congratulating me on my good work! One woman asked me if I would go and serve her church. *That's a bit much*, I thought. After all, I was still shell-shocked from the ordeal. I might have come through it unscathed, but I was still feeling raw from the trauma of being thrown on the platform as a complete novice.

Despite the initial trauma, getting over that first hurdle of public mediumship lifted me to a great height. It felt as though I had walked across a high wire with no net beneath me – one slip and I might never have found the courage to attempt it again. As it was, I could now afford to look over my shoulder and see the gap of doubt bridged. Now I felt more trusting of the spirit friends who had impressed me all my life.

Before that night, my only experience of speaking in public had been reading the odd poem or passage in church. But when you are asked to demonstrate as a medium, you have no script whatsoever. You really do go out on a limb. All you have is trust – trust in a spirit world that you know exists and the trust of those who come to witness your gift. It is at this point, where trust of the medium and need of the people become one, that spirit communication occurs.

Now I had the problem of telling Mrs Primrose. I thought she would go mad, as she never allowed anyone on a platform before they were given her seal of approval. To my surprise, she was philosophical. 'Well, it was bound to happen sooner or later,' she said. 'And besides, all the reports I've heard have been very good. I just wish I'd been there to watch.'

Afterwards Mrs Primrose told me she had always known I would be a platform medium and that it was just as well she had not been in the church that night otherwise I might have waited years to go on the platform. But she suggested I should work with her for a while, taking half the service while she took the other half. This we did four times in succession, and after that I was on my own. At first, I worked only in our church, but it was not too long before I was asked to demonstrate in some of the others around Glasgow.

When I began as a working medium, every

time I was as nervous as I had been on my first night. Each new church I visited brought a fresh bout of nerves. In fact I would be a nervous wreck a whole week before I was due to appear. Whenever I finished a service and people approached me to say how well I had done or to thank me for a message I had given them, I would try to act quite cool and aloof, as if I had been doing this for years. But really I must have looked like a frightened rabbit. I would be soaking with perspiration and shaking like a leaf, only too glad to have got it over with.

In the first year I worked on the platform only two spirit contacts I gave stand out in my mind. Each is very different, but together they sum up my brand of mediumship.

The first happened in a small church not too far from Glasgow. I was working away quite well when my attention turned to an elderly lady sitting to my left, a pleasant-looking woman with a lovely smile on her face. When I said, 'Can I speak to you, dear?', she replied, 'Oh, yes.' I proceeded to inform her that her mother was with her. The communicator said her name was Cathy, that she had passed on in 1969 and that she was with Mr Thompson.

'Oh, young man, that is so nice,' said the lady, quite delighted. 'You see, Cathy is my mum and Thompson was our family name. That'll be my dad she's with. Oh, lovely!'

Everything was going fine until I added, 'I also

have a man here by the name of Joe, who says…' I was just in the middle of my sentence when the woman screamed at me, 'Well, you can just bloody well send him back to the snake pit he's crawled out of!'

'But, madam…'

I couldn't get a word in by this point.

'If he thinks for one bloomin' minute that I have anything to say to him,' she was saying, 'he's up a bloody gum tree!' On and on she went, finishing with, 'The day that ratbag died was the happiest of my life!'

By this stage, I couldn't stop laughing and was joined by the whole congregation who, it turned out, knew the woman's story. It seemed that she had been given a very hard time by her husband when he was alive and had celebrated when he died! On previous occasions other mediums had given messages from her parents and so on, but I was the first to allow Joseph the Terrible to contact her from the Other Side. He was only there to beg her forgiveness, but the choice was hers. If she didn't wish to grant it, that was up to her. Who are we to judge? Back he jolly well scuttled to his realm of guilt and remorse.

After the service was over, the woman came to me and apologized for her outburst, saying, 'Do you know, son, I really couldn't stand that man. It wasn't until I got my first pair of glasses that I saw what I had married. He was vile. He was also very bad to me. I don't know if I'll ever forgive him, but at least he gave us all a laugh tonight. That's something, I suppose.'

I still get a laugh when I share that story with people.

The second memorable message is in total contrast to the first, but it still managed to strike an emotional chord in the recipient's heart.

I was working in a Spiritualist church on the west coast of Scotland one Sunday afternoon and was passing a message to an elderly gentleman from his dear wife in the spirit world when I became aware of a spirit presence almost leaning against me. There seemed to be a real urgency with this soul waiting to communicate. It was a middle-aged woman of about medium height and build, with short brown hair. I sent a thought to her that she would have to wait while at the same time continuing to speak to the gentleman I was dealing with. Mediums' ability to speak to someone and at the same time hold several conversations in their mind with spirit people is an art form in itself.

Eventually I concluded the message at hand and asked the spirit lady whom her message was for. Immediately, she drew my attention to a young lady at the back of the church.

'That is my daughter,' she said. I could hear the voice so clearly in my head it was as if she were actually inside me. Now it was up to me to trust her and pass on her message as best I could.

'Young lady at the back of the hall, may I speak with you?' I asked.

'Yes,' came the reply, rather quietly.

'There is a lady here who says that you are her daughter. Is that correct?'

'Yes.'

This time she spoke with much more vigour. At this point, the message came pouring through.

'Your mother says her name is Sarah. She also says that she has only been over a short while, maybe nine or ten months. Is that correct?'

This information appeared to be right. Sarah prompted me further to say, 'Tell Caroline I will be with her on 3 October and also that her little girl will be fine.'

I had to ask, 'Is your name Caroline?'

'Yes, it is.'

'Well, Sarah says that she will be with you on 3 October and also that your little girl will be fine.'

With this message delivered, the intensity that I was feeling from Sarah began to ease off. The last point she asked me to relay to her now very tearful daughter was that her father was with her in the spirit world. His name was William and they would both be looking after their daughter from the Other Side.

At the close of the service Caroline came to thank me for the message she had received. She told me that her mother had died ten months previously of breast cancer, aged just 44, and her father had passed away five years earlier in a motor accident. *My God*, I thought, *what loss for someone so young.*

It turned out that Caroline had just come along to see what a Spiritualist service was like, but in her heart hoped that her mother might communicate once the demonstration began. She then told me she was due to have a baby in November and that she wished that her mother could be with her at that time. I said I was sure that she would be, then told her to keep in mind the date her mother had passed to her.

As I looked at Caroline's face I felt as though I had really helped someone that night. She asked me when I would be serving this church in the future and I told her it would not be until December. 'I hope to see you then,' she said. 'Thanks again.' And with that she left.

When I returned to the church later in the year, there to meet me at the door was Caroline, together with her new baby in her arms. 'I couldn't wait to see you,' she said, her voice filled with excitement. 'My mother was right, she was so right.'

It took me a moment to comprehend what she was trying to tell me. 'My daughter was born on 3 October,' she explained. 'She was premature by one month, but as Mum said, she's fine.' What's more, baby Sarah had been named (Spiritualism's alternative to baptism) at the Spiritualist church the previous week.

When you see people lifted out of despair because of something you have been allowed to do for them, it makes you feel humble, especially when it is someone so young, with so much life ahead of them. Mediumship really can help people to come through their grief with less pain than is normally experienced at such times. After all, our message is that there is life after death. I can only hope that what I do as a medium will allow people to get on with their lives in a constructive and more positive way.

By now, my work as a medium had truly begun. More and more of my time would be given to this aspect of my life.

CHAPTER FIVE

Working as a medium in the early days, I was eager to demonstrate wherever I was invited and travelled around all the local Spiritualist churches. I was so intense in those days. The whole business seemed to be dead serious – no pun intended! – but looking back I can see the humour in so many situations.

One night, driving along the motorway to a church in Wishaw, approximately 20 miles south-east of Glasgow, I suddenly realized I was on the wrong road. Chrissie, the church President, was to meet me at a roundabout just off another motorway, at the Motherwell turnoff. But by the time I'd changed motorways and eventually found the right round-about, she'd gone, probably thinking I wasn't coming.

Having arranged to be met, I hadn't thought to ask the address of the church. All I knew was that the meetings were being held in the local

Scout hall until they were able to move into their new premises. A flash of inspiration hit me: I would go to the local police station and ask where the Scout hall was.

By now I was running about ten minutes late. *Still time to do most of the service*, I thought. After I managed to obtain directions from one of the locals, I drove to the police station, parked the car hurriedly, ran through the pouring rain, threw open the door and said in a desperate voice, 'I need to find the local Scout hall.'

The desk sergeant took one look at me, standing there in my long raincoat panting like some sort of raving pervert, and said in a suspicious tone, 'Now why would that be, young man?'

All of a sudden it hit me what I must have looked like. How was I to explain to this policeman that I was a medium and should be taking a service for the Wishaw Spiritualist group?

As briefly as I could, I told him of my predicament. He gave a dry smile and said, 'You would think that with you being a medium and all that, you would be able to ask for divine guidance.' But in spite of the unoriginal comment, he finally gave me directions and I sped off thankfully.

When I arrived at the small wooden hall, I could see the shadows of the crowd assembled inside. It looked as if they had all just sat down in unison.

'Thank God,' I said to myself. 'Chrissie must

have known that I wouldn't let her down. They haven't actually started yet.'

I hurried into the main room and said in my most apologetic voice, 'I'm so sorry I'm late, but I started out on the wrong motorway.'

The people looked somewhat surprised to see me. A man standing on a small stage turned to me and asked who I was.

'Gordon Smith,' I replied, hoping this would mean something.

'But why are you here?'

'I'm the medium,' I began. Then a horrible feeling ran through me, for from the corner of my eye I could see a sign that read: 'JESUS SAVES ALL SINNERS.' *Oh dear*, I thought. I had stumbled into a born-again Christian meeting! Before anyone could say another word, I was out of there, legging it back to the car and heading for home.

What an ordeal! I was soaked, exasperated and downright fed up. When I arrived home, I phoned Chrissie and told her of my plight. She laughed her head off, because the hall I went to had been the correct one about two weeks previously, but the born-again people had had the Spiritualists thrown out.

I now look back at this farce with great delight, although I am sure that if I had hung about I would have been thrown to the lions. This experience taught me two valuable lessons. The first is always to get proper directions when travelling to a church. The second is never to wear a raincoat when looking for a local Scout hut in a strange town. Good advice for any aspiring medium about to tour the church circuit for the first time…

Working the small churches around Glasgow was the best apprenticeship any medium could wish for. The people in these churches were down to earth and straight to the point. On a few occasions I was even sworn at. The truth sometimes hurts, but there is still no greater teacher. Some of my best work came from these humble little churches. God bless all who keep their doors open.

By now, I was gaining quite a reputation as a competent medium around the west of Scotland and offers were coming in for me to work further afield. As well as this, I had a mountain of requests for private sittings. Typically, I tried to do everything and once again I was told by Mrs Primrose: 'Nil by mind.' It was now right for me to take some time for myself, away from Spiritualist churches and mediumship of any description.

This was the best thing I could have done, for somewhere in the last two years I had lost all touch with reality. My entire life was in disarray. I had been running all over the place trying to please everyone and somehow forgotten about myself. It felt as though I had drifted away from the people that I would share a drink with in the local pub, and even though my family and closest friends were aware of what I was now doing, many would avoid any kind of conversation that involved death, dying or the afterlife.

Sensitivity is the one aspect of mediumship that has to be tuned to perfection. It is a medium's sensitive nature that becomes enhanced in spiritual development, but the danger is that it can encroach on everyday life if not properly controlled. As my sensitivity began to heighten more and more, it became important to learn to control it, otherwise things would appear larger than life. Let me try to explain it like this. In daily life, things appear as normal. You might look at your face in a mirror one day and notice a small pimple. When your sensitivity is heightened, that same small spot will appear as a face full of acne. Everything in your life becomes exaggerated; you begin to see molehills as mountains. It is very difficult to keep a balance between the spiritual and the material when your sensitivity first starts to expand.

It is very important to normalize yourself. Learning to switch off mediumship is essential. I have learned to ground myself by doing ordinary things like cleaning the car or washing windows at home. Nowadays, whenever things really become too much for me, I take myself off into the countryside and walk for miles or sit by a waterfall or loch, anywhere that I can find peace and stillness. I walk in the country as often as I can and always feel replenished and relaxed after my visits to Mother

Nature's garden.

The year of 1992 was coming to a close. I had now been in my development circle for more than five years and for the last 18 months or so had served churches as a medium. I had taken one month away from the spirit world and felt good in myself. I had done some soul-searching and realized that I had to learn to say 'No!' more often. From now on, I would let my spirit friends advise me about which churches to serve and ask for their guidance about giving private sittings.

This is a great system provided that the medium keeps to it, but as soon as I started back, I was off again on the roller-coaster. In the coming year, I found that I had even more engagements for churches, whilst my diary was full to bursting with appointments for private sittings. It is the easiest thing in the world deciding you will say 'No'… until the phone rings!

One day while working in the hairdressing salon, I received a telephone call from a distraught woman. She was crying and saying that she had to speak to the medium Gordon Smith. I told her I was at work, but promised I would call back if she left me a number.

After the day's work was over, I called and arranged to see her the following day, which was my day off. I instructed her not to supply any information about her life or situation, which is something I always do when asked to give private sittings to strangers. After returning and settling down to watch some television, I drifted into a snooze.

Although not in a deep sleep, I began to dream. In the dream I saw a man in his mid-twenties. He was reasonably tall with short blond hair. He was running as if he were late for something, but then for no apparent reason he fell down. This short dream played over several times in my mind until I began to stir.

When I opened my eyes, I could see the same man standing beside me, only he was not all there. By this, I mean he was visible only from the waist up. Then he communicated something without actually speaking: 'Francis John.' Just the name, and he was gone. For the rest of the night, I asked my spirit helpers who this young man was, but it seemed that the lines were down. I was given no reply and decided to put it down to experience.

The following morning, after a light breakfast I headed off early to sit for the distraught lady of the previous day. When I finally reached the address I had been given, I was greeted by a man in his mid-forties. He showed me into the living-room, where I was introduced to Mrs Preston, the lady I had spoken to. She was also in her mid-forties, I would have said, with shoulder-length dark curly hair. She was very slim and there was a deep sadness in her dark brown eyes.

After a short introduction and a brief rundown

of how a private sitting works, I got started. The very second that I took Mrs Preston's hand, I could hear the voice of a spirit gentleman clearly in my left ear. 'Mum, Mum, I'm here,' he whispered.

As I passed this information to Mrs Preston, she instantly began to cry. At this point, I closed my eyes and saw the face of the young man I had seen the night before uttering the name 'Francis John'. Then something happened that had never occurred to me before in a private sitting – I could feel myself going into trance. I will let Mrs Preston tell the rest:

I had never had a sitting with a medium before. When Gordon entered my home, I was a bit taken aback by how young he was. I really expected someone older. However, once he spoke to me and settled my fears, I felt quite safe in his hands. Gordon took my hand and then mentioned the words 'Mum, I'm here', after which he told me my son's proper name, Francis John, which is what he was christened, although he was known as Franky.

Gordon said at the outset of the sitting that he would not go into any funny trance states, although that is exactly what he did. When his eyes closed, he remained quiet for a while and then a voice quite different from his own spoke through him.

I was told that my son was safe and that he

did not feel a thing when he passed away. I was then told the exact date that he had died, which was ten days before this, on the eighteenth. It then became clear that my son was influencing the voice that was speaking, as he said things in a way that only he could.

My heart began to fill with joy as this discourse continued. Franky had been married for just over a year when tragedy struck. His young widow was called Christine. During this session he said, 'Tell Chris to remember the Lake District.' This is where they spent their honeymoon. He then sent his regards to the rest of his family, each by their first name.

The amount of information that came through to me was all relevant to the life of my son and to the life of my family. At the end of this session, Franky told me if I ever wanted to see him, I should look for the brightest star in the sky. This is what I would say to him when as a child he would ask where his grandpa went after he died. I always said to him, 'Look for the brightest star in the sky, Franky. That is where your grandpa is.'

I don't know what prompted me to have a sitting with a medium, but what I do know is that I have spoken to my son in Heaven and he sounded happy. I just want to thank Gordon so much for his very special gift. I hope that God will take care of him so he may *be able to bring comfort to others who have suffered as our family have.*

At the end of this experience, I learned that I had been sitting for slightly more than an hour, even though it had only seemed like seconds to me. When the story was relayed back to me, I was quite astonished. Mrs Preston could not thank me enough, saying she felt that great pain had been lifted from her and that there was a lightness about her that she had not felt since she had been given the terrible news of her son.

When I arrived home later that day, I still couldn't comprehend what had happened. My sensitivity had expanded so much that I just couldn't believe it. But when you sit for someone who genuinely requires a proper contact with the spirit world, the guides and helpers on the Other Side do pull out all the stops. In this particular case, there was so much unfinished business that I believe my spirit friends definitely inspired the sitting.

The only thing about working at this level is that soon I found myself in constant demand. So much for saying 'No'!

CHAPTER SIX

It was January 1995. The Glasgow Association of Spiritualists was about to celebrate its 130th anniversary. The celebration was to be headed by two mediums giving a double demonstration of clairvoyance. I was invited to share the platform with Albert Best.

The prospect left me with mixed feelings. On one hand, I was filled with pride at the thought of working with such a highly revered clairvoyant as Albert. On the other, I was terrified that I might not measure up to this great exponent of mediumship.

Before the service, we shared nervous small talk. Mr Best, I imagine, was trying to work out why this medium almost unknown to him had been invited to demonstrate on such a special evening. He asked me where I had worked before. Hesitantly, I mentioned a few of the bigger churches in which I had demonstrated, but I don't think he was impressed at all, as he had appeared all over the world.

'Everywhere except for Japan,' he said. 'But you will work there within the next five years.' Of course I took this throwaway prediction with a pinch of salt.

We walked out together to face a rather overcrowded church. Two hundred and fifty people had squeezed into the place, which can take up to 230 at a push. Outside there were a further 50 or so who had to be turned away. Every time Albert was announced in a church this was the typical scene. It had nothing to do with me. I felt like the support act that goes on before the main attraction to warm up the crowd. Fortunately, as I completed my work, Albert walked forward to the microphone and announced, 'What we have just witnessed is a young medium who has the potential to be an excellent medium.'

Albert couldn't believe that I worked the way I did. Later, he said to me, 'I was becoming sick of being told about all these so-called "brilliant new mediums".' He had seen many who, in his opinion, turned out to speak well, but gave very general information to people. 'It was good to see someone who could actually do the work properly,' he added. This meant so much to me at the time, and still does.

Mediumship was Albert's life and he was

always completely sincere with people. He had no time for those who were playing games with the subject and felt even more strongly about the way some Spiritualist organizations were training mediums. So from that night forward he decided to take me under his wing. What a great honour indeed.

Albert Best taught me more about mediumship in two years than most mediums will learn in 20. Like Mrs Primrose, my previous teacher, he was not a great philosopher. No, it was more to do with his own life experience. His greatest attributes were humility and complete lack of ego. Albert gave private sittings to some of the most famous people in the world, yet he never mentioned them. I still have some of his photo albums. They contain hundreds of signed photographs of pop stars, famous actors, politicians and royalty from every part of the globe, all thanking this honourable little Irishman for his kindness. If ever I asked about one or other of them, Albert would simply say, 'Oh, they are just people who need help like anyone else.'

This is how mediums should conduct their mediumship. Today, if a celebrity has a sitting with a medium or psychic, an account of their private life is normally splashed over the front pages of one of the daily newspapers soon afterwards. This is shortly followed up with a book about the medium's life. Yet the ethics of spiritual mediumship should never allow any genuine clairvoyant to divulge the private information between themselves and their client for a quick buck.

People like Albert and Mrs Primrose were decent and down to earth. The only real teaching they gave was by example. What made them good was the fact that they had known great suffering in their lives. But more than this, they were both driven to prevent the suffering of any other being in this world. The true act of mediumship is born of compassion.

After this, I made a point of visiting Albert two or three days each week. As he lived by himself, my friend Jim McManus or I would spent time with him at his flat on the south side of Glasgow. Albert was very independent and always fussed when we offered to cut his hair or take him to hospital for check-ups. He insisted on trying to give us things. Of course I would accept nothing from him. This always led to great battles between us.

At this point in his life, Albert's mobility was very poor. Indeed, the demonstration of clairvoyance we shared in January that year was to be the last time he worked in Scotland. Here was this poor old soul, near to the end of his life, a life in which he had given so much of his time to so many others and had asked for nothing. I know for a fact that he appreciated the times we spent together. His pale blue eyes would light up whenever I entered his home. He was excited to hear all about my work in the churches and just as eager to know the gossip.

Albert was keen for me to work in all the

most reputable Spiritualist centres around the country and the fact that it was Albert who recommended me made people within the Spiritualist movement take notice, as the great Mr Best had never been known to promote a medium before. Albert certainly had an effect on my life, not only in the psychic field, but more importantly, on my whole attitude to life and the way I viewed other people. This altered dramatically just listening to the events of his life and watching his face go through a spectrum of emotional changes as he shared some of the brilliant episodes of his incredible journey with me. It made me feel much more responsible for those who sought comfort from my mediumship. Because of Albert, I would have to say that I truly developed a much deeper understanding of people. I can never emulate this supreme medium. Even to try would be wrong, but if I can fulfil the potential he saw in me, I know he will smile down on me from Heaven.

The last time I shared a conversation with Albert, Jim and I had just had lunch with him in town. We drove back to his new flat, which was part of a sheltered housing complex, The three of us were talking about a trip that I was soon to make to Yorkshire for a seminar on Spiritualism when someone knocked at the door.

Jim answered the door to a very refined lady wishing to speak to Mr Best. Albert introduced her to both Jim and me – but the strange thing was that he announced us as two plain-clothes policemen! Albert was such a practical joker that the pair of us went along with it. The lady seemed to be none the wiser. Within a few moments of our strange introduction, Jim and I left her to speak to Albert in private. On the way home we discussed this bizarre episode, not fully understanding the intent behind it. But with Albert you just never knew.

The following day I headed off to my seminar in Yorkshire. Whilst I was there, I had a strange feeling that something was wrong with Albert. I phoned home, only to be told he was fine and that I shouldn't worry about him so much.

When I eventually did get home at the end of the week, Jim informed me that Albert was in hospital in a coma. Immediately, I rushed to see him. He was attached to a drip and not conscious. For the next ten days his condition remained the same. Each night either Jim or I went to visit him to see if his condition had changed in any way, and his dear friend Ann Docherty was almost constantly by his bedside. Ann looked after him well and had been a close friend of his for many years.

One particular evening, Jim and I walked into the ward as usual. Ann was standing at the head of the bed, stroking Albert's forehead. I joined her at the right-hand side of the bed as Jim made his way around to the left of Albert.

The three of us stood there in silence, looking down on our dear old friend. I guess it must have been at the end of the visit that I began to sense a lady with long auburn hair standing at the foot of the bed. I knew that no one could see her as she was obviously from the spirit world.

I looked across to Jim and then to Ann, for by now there seemed to be a feeling of intensity building around us. Then Albert began to stir. Still in silence, we all looked directly at him, not knowing what to expect.

Albert's eyes opened. He looked at each one of us in turn, starting with Jim, who was holding his left hand. Then he turned his head to me and eventually to Ann. Lifting his head from the pillow, he fixed his eyes on the foot of his bed. By now the spirit lady had become so obvious that I imagined the others might be aware of her presence. As if in a trance, Albert's eyes widened and began to fill with tears. A huge smile broke over his face as he tried to pull himself up further. Still smiling, with teardrops running down his cheeks, he said softly, 'My wife is here.' Both Ann and Jim turned their heads to the foot of his bed. 'And my children – they've come for me.' The three of us were fighting back tears. 'You'll have to let me go,' he whispered.

I could not hold back my tears another moment. The feeling of joy that was emanating from Albert was indescribable. Ann leaned down toward him and said, 'We were never holding you, Albert.'

With this, he closed his eyes and shortly

afterwards was with his wife and children, whom he had not held for 50 years or so, as they had died in the Second World War. God bless them all.

Albert left instructions with Ann that he wanted no funeral. He donated his body to medical research. Even in death his wish was that other people might benefit, which was typical of this special man.

As there wasn't a funeral service, Ann, Jim and I set about arranging a service of thanksgiving for the life of Albert Best. So many people wanted to attend that we had to use the large church hall at the Glasgow Association of Spiritualists to accommodate the crowds. Tributes were sent from all over the world. All in all, I would say that the service was a great success. The only mishap was discovered when the sound engineer, who was there to tape the proceedings, found that not one word or sound had been recorded, even after he had made several checks.

At the service, the crowded church listened to the adventures of this humble man. Each of his great journeys offered stories of miraculous healings or wonderful messages filled with hope and love. Albert loved to laugh, so we kept the whole affair lighthearted. Many funny tales were shared by those who knew Albert as a clown, the role that he loved to play for others. He was never happier than when making others laugh at his expense.

Eric Hatton, then President of the United Kingdom's Spiritualists' National Union, told of how Albert, returning home late from a trip, found that one of his friends had been in his flat and left some food out for him. What he didn't know was that the kindly soul had decided to varnish the rather tatty wooden toilet seat as well. The unsuspecting Albert found the need to use the shiny new-looking toilet furnishing … and on doing so was completely and utterly stuck.

After screaming out for an hour, he was rescued by his elderly female neighbour, whom he instructed to call an ambulance. The two ambulance men who escorted him to the hospital took great delight in making jokes about his predicament. But it was the doctor in the casualty department who added the crowning glory to this good deed gone wrong.

Albert, now lying face down on a trolley with the offending object fastened firmly to his bare rump, said, 'I bet you've not seen one of these before, doctor.'

'Yes, in fact I see them every day,' he replied. 'But I must admit I have never seen one framed before!'

As this story was recited, I could almost hear the little Irishman's laughter from the spirit world.

CHAPTER SEVEN

Don't get me wrong – I don't make fun of mediums or Spiritualism, especially when true and sincere exponents of it are helping many people who really do need support at difficult times in their lives. But humorous situations do sometimes arise when people are trying desperately to be serious.

One of Albert Best's greatest features was his ability to laugh at himself and some of the ridiculous situations he found himself in. He told me the following story. He had just sat down after demonstrating his unique gift of clairvoyance to a packed London church when his very gracious Chair arose to thank him and to inform the congregation that Albert would be available for private sittings the following day. What she actually said was, 'Ladies and gentlemen, I am sure you will all join with me in thanking Mr Best for his excellent demonstration of mediumship. Furthermore, I take great delight in announcing that Albert will be holding his privates for three hours tomorrow morning. If anyone would like to book a session with him, please see me at the close of the service.'

Albert told me he had a vision of himself cupping his 'privates' and charging ten pounds for half-hour sessions! What made this even funnier was that the Chair didn't realize her mistake, much to everyone's delight.

Another hilarious slip of the tongue occurred at our development circle in West Princes Street one Thursday night. At the end of a circle, the leader asks each person if they have a message for anyone else in the group. On this particular evening, one lady got to her feet and approached the gentleman sitting opposite her, who was wearing a very obvious wig.

'When I looked at you,' she said, apparently unable to take her eyes off his thick black scalp furnishing, 'I was aware of North American Indians dancing around you.' Still looking at the wig, she added, 'Then there was a great scene of the whole tribe.'

'The whole tribe,' the man repeated rather doubtfully.

'Yes,' she replied. 'They were dancing around a toupee.'

Everybody in the room tried to muffle their

laughter, hoping not to embarrass the poor man. But as quick as a flash, he came back with: 'I think, my dear, that the word you are looking for is "teepee". But thank you for your message. The Indian you saw must be the one who scalped me.'

The entire room erupted with laughter, as you can imagine. Some of the funniest things in life seem to arise out of embarrassing situations, though in this case I'm not sure who was the more embarrassed in the end!

One idea that has always aroused interest amongst Spiritualists is that of having your own spirit guide. The very thought of someone watching over you is comforting, but the way some people describe their spirit guides can be quite hilarious, especially when you add a generous slice of Glasgow patter.

I was sitting in the tearoom of a Spiritualist church in the East End of Glasgow one Sunday evening at the end of the service when I overheard a conversation between a couple of elderly ladies. I will call the first lady Jeannie and the second Betty.

Jeannie: 'Hey, Betty, see your guide. He's a big stouter, so he is.'

Betty: 'Aye, 'e's some size a man, in't 'e?'

Jeannie: 'It's no rat. It's the size o' 'is weapon.'

Betty: 'Aye, yur right. It's a cracker. I've held it, so ah huv. An' did ye see 'is feathurs?'

Jeannie: 'Oh, they wur beautiful, so they wur. He wiz covered in thum. Heed tae fit.'

Betty: 'Some o' these Indians ur magnificent specimens of manhood, so they ur.'

Jeannie: 'Well, ah don't know how a wee wumin like yursel kin let a big man like rat cum throo' 'ur.'

Betty: 'Ach, wance ye get usedntae it, it's no rat bad, ne'er it is. Beside a' ma guides ur big men.'

Jeannie: 'Oh, you're dead lucky, you ur, mine ur aw wee wumen.'

I wonder what the guides were discussing while this conversation was taking place. Perhaps they were comparing weapons!

Tricia Robertson, of the Scottish Society for Psychical Research, told me a funny thing that happened when she and Professor Archie Roy were asked to investigate a pub in Glasgow. Apparently most of the bar staff had experienced eerie feelings in certain parts of the public house and after many complaints the manager had finally agreed to call in the psychical researchers.

The only time that Tricia and Archie had available to investigate this 'haunting' was Friday around lunchtime. You can imagine how busy the bar was. Having been advised by the manager to be discreet about their investigations, Tricia told Archie to have a seat in the corner out of the way while she had a quiet word with the man in charge. As she pushed her way through the packed bar, she managed to catch the attention of one of the staff, a young woman whose mind was occupied with large orders for drinks. 'What, hen?' she shouted to Tricia over the noise of the crowded bar room.

Tricia, trying her best to be discreet, said, 'I'm here about the disturbance.'

'Aw, hen, you're in a pub. People are allowed to make noise,' the barmaid answered.

'No,' Tricia said, trying her utmost not to give the game away to all the customers, 'Professor Roy and I have been called in by the manager to help with the other disturbances.'

She winked at the bemused girl and suddenly the penny dropped. 'Just a wee minute, pet. I'll get the boss,' the barmaid said. Putting down the pints of beer she was holding, she cupped her hands around her mouth and shouted as loudly as possible, 'Sammy, it's the people about the ghost!'

Instantly, the whole bar fell silent. The manager dropped his head into his hands in horror. Well, I would say that this was the time for a sharp exit, wouldn't you?

One funny thing that I witnessed personally was when a visiting healer asked to be allowed to work with our own church healers one night. After he had given his credentials and a rather long lecture on his experience, he was invited to work alongside our regular healers and chose to treat a man already waiting in the dimly lit room.

During the healing, the patient tried to

protest that the healer was working on the wrong area of his body. 'It's not that leg,' he said.

'Just keep quiet. I know what I'm doing,' replied the healer. 'In fact, I am a specialist in healing legs. The spirit doctor that works with me has performed many spirit operations on the best athletes in the country.'

He continued with the healing and it was not until the session was over and the lights had been switched on that everyone realized that the leg that had been 'treated' for over half an hour was wooden!

I couldn't help but say to the friend sitting beside me, 'I don't care how long he works on the patient, but that leg is definitely not coming back!'

Isn't it just ironic that those who profess to be great at their particular craft always seem to come unstuck, and usually in front of the very people they are trying to impress?

Spiritualism certainly attracts some strange individuals from time to time, as I am sure most religions do. One Thursday evening the topic for discussion was how knowledge of the Spirit had brought joy into our lives. A very well-groomed lady who was attending church for the first time stood up and announced: 'I have a spirit gentleman in my house and each night when I go to bed he makes love to me.'

Now, what did she expect me to say to that? I had no idea. 'Is this something you would like us to investigate?' I enquired. She looked at me blankly. 'I mean, I'm sure you are very distressed about this,' I continued, but she stopped me in mid-sentence. 'Absolutely not, young man. I just wanted to let you all know how happy the spirit world has made me. After all, that is what you are discussing, is it not?'

I've said it before and I'll say it again: 'There's nowt so queer as folk.'

In fact, when I think of some of the things that mediums have to put up with – and in our own churches! – all I can say is that you have to develop two things: a very thick skin and a bizarre sense of humour. Often humour appears more frequently than the spirit people do! As entertaining as it all seems, though, it must never distract from the serious business, although I am certain that those on the Other Side get such a laugh at us trying ever so hard to be spiritual.

It is my belief, though, that your spiritual journey should include fun. It has been the joy I have experienced in my development that has kept me on the spiritual path. This life can be so hard that there are times when this sense of joy eludes us. So whenever you get the chance to be happy, reach out and grasp it with both hands.

CHAPTER EIGHT

Many people consider mediums to be rather strange. I don't see myself that way, although some of the episodes in my life since developing my mediumship have been bizarre, to say the least. If anyone had told me I would end up in some of the places I have been to or meet some of the people I've encountered, I would have told them they were out of their minds. I was brought up in a working-class area of Glasgow and had only average academic ability. Nowadays I find myself being invited to speak before a packed lecture theatre of academics in Glasgow University or to visit large country estates to teach at seminars and conferences. Sometimes I have to pinch myself to realize I'm not dreaming. On the other hand, there are times I wish I were dreaming!

One of the most ridiculous requests ever

made to me as a medium came out of the blue. I was working in the salon late one Friday afternoon. It was a typical day at City Barbers. Shouts of 'Next!' came from all corners of the busy salon.

'How dae ye wnt yur herr cut?'

'A short back and sides, please.'

'Is 'at a number wan ur a number two?' referring to the level of the electric clippers.

By this time of day the staff had lost most of their affability and everyone's intention was either to get home or to the pub.

'Gordon, phone!' one of the staff bellowed.

The voice on the other end of the phone was that of a foreign lady, requesting that I join her immediately in the Hilton Hotel, where she would be for the next four hours. There seemed to be no way to explain to her that I was at work and would have to get permission from my boss to leave early. 'Tell your boss man to send you to me and I will pay your wages,' she said. After a few more words between her, my boss and me, it was agreed I would be released early.

Try to imagine how I felt when I approached the front entrance of the Glasgow Hilton in my working clothes. I certainly got some looks from the high-class clientele, all dressed for dinner, as I walked through the grand lobby.

'Are you sure you are in the right place, sir?' the elderly concierge asked me in a patronizing tone.

'Yes,' I replied. 'I am expected by Madam X in Room 1108, thank you very much.'

It was at this point I realized the anonymous lady must be of importance as the concierge almost fell backwards in disbelief.

The door of the room was opened and in front of me was a beautiful middle-aged woman whom I instantly recognized. This time it was me who almost fell backwards.

'Please come in, Mr Smith,' she said, motioning me into the room. Her tone was more gracious now than it had been before. 'Thank you so much for seeing me at such short notice,' she said gently.

All I could do was to stare, but eventually I pulled myself together, for I was here to give this lady a private sitting. Almost as soon as I tuned in, the spirit people came though and spoke to her. During this I forgot she was someone of importance.

After giving evidence from her loved ones on the Other Side for almost an hour, I paused for a moment and asked my sitter if she had any questions.

'Yes, I do,' she said, frowning at me. 'I need you to ask your spirit people if they can assist my husband.'

'In what way, madam?'

'Well, it looks as if there is going to be a great public scandal concerning my husband. What I want you to do is to ask the spirits to influence some people's minds so that it... '

'I am very sorry,' I stopped her in mid-sentence.

'I can't do such things.'

'I know it might sound a little bit immoral, but I will pay you well.'

'Madam,' I said, 'you don't seem to understand me. When I said I couldn't do it, it's not because of any immorality. The fact is, I don't have the power to do it.'

'But you speak to them. Won't they help me if you ask them on my behalf? I mean, my husband could be ruined if you don't.'

I really couldn't believe this. Here was this high-powered lady whose husband held a very important position in the running of their country, pleading with little me to call on the spirit world to sort out an impending scandal! The only thing I could offer her was prayer, although some kind of counselling might not have gone amiss.

'I will ask for prayers to be said for both you and your husband,' I promised. 'If it is God's will, then nothing will come of the other matter.' It is not too difficult to see how Rasputin misguided the Romanovs!

Fortunately, I never heard anything more of that particular scandal. I guess the prayers did the job – or, if not, a hefty payoff! Needless to say, I still get calls from Madam X when her country is in need of – prayers, shall we say?

The more aware I become, the more paranormal activities I discover going on around me. I have always been fascinated by the predictions that have followed me through life. Words like 'coincidence' are no longer sufficient when the evidence is supported by fact. The following account is not so much strange but true – and it is nice!

Dronma, my Tibetan Buddhist friend, is a very gifted psychic artist. In our development circle, she sometimes tunes in and draws a spirit person who wishes to be sketched. On the evening of 8 December 1995, she was showing us some drawings of spirit people. Then she said, 'Oh yes, this one,' turning the page of the sketch-pad. 'I don't know why I drew this at all.'

It was a detailed drawing of a springer spaniel pup. After we all agreed how cute the little dog was, Dronma said, 'I don't think this is a spirit dog. This little thing is seen in the drawing sitting at your door, Gordon.' In fact, the door behind the dog was similar to mine. Before we moved on to the next drawing, Dronma told me to look at the little barrel hanging from the dog's collar. 'Although it is a pencil drawing, I feel that the little barrel is red,' she said. She then dated the page, as she does with all her drawings, and that was it.

Almost nine months later, I received a call from my good friend June Oakley, an excellent clairvoyant who lives in Leicester. Occasionally June and I chat on the phone, keeping each other up to date with what is going on either side of the border. Out of the blue, June said to me, 'Gordon, you are going to be offered a pup. It's a spaniel pup. I am being told by my friends in the spirit world that you must accept this little dog.'

'Well, June,' I joked, 'whoever is telling you this had better find another home for it because there's no way I can have a dog at this time.'

'Oh well, dear, that's what they said,' June finished.

A week later, after I had been speaking at a seminar in Glasgow, a lady approached me, asking if I knew of anyone who would be willing to give a little dog a good home. 'It's just that he will be put back in the dogs' home if no one takes him soon,' she said woefully.

I apologized for not being of any assistance and then suddenly remembered my telephone conversation with June.

'Wait,' I called after the lady, who had started to walk away. 'Is this dog a spaniel?'

'Yes, as a matter of fact it is,' she said.

I made an appointment to go to see the dog with the agreement that if he were friendly, I would consider taking him home with me.

Typically, as soon as I cast my eyes on this energetic ball of fur, with his long ears and sad, cheeky face, I had to have him. His name is Charlie and most people refer to him as Cheeky Charlie. I must admit he hasn't been the easiest of pets to break in. It was because he was so lively that his previous owners wanted to get rid of him. They were the third owners in his nine months of existence. But after he had eaten a hall carpet and chewed his way through a door and just about every shoe in the house, Cheeky Charlie finally began to settle, thank God.

About a month after he arrived, his kennel papers were sent to me, along with all his veterinary records. When I was going over the papers, I noticed that he was born on 8 December 1995 – the very day that Dronma drew the little springer in our circle. Further confirmation was that hanging from the dog's collar was a little red barrel. So I suppose that Charlie is not only a dog, but also a living prediction that I am now so glad came true. Maybe I should have changed his name to Déjà Vu!

Have you ever tried to help someone, only to find that the assistance you gave caused more trouble than it was worth? Well, that is what happened to me when I tried to locate a diamond bracelet.

I had just arrived at work one morning when the lady who owned the newsagent's shop across the street asked if I could give her a moment of my time. Not really knowing what to expect, I agreed. When I walked through the door of the small shop, I was greeted by her husband, a rather intent-looking man in his early forties. As I approached him, he dropped his eyelids in a gesture of disgust and motioned me into the back of the shop, where his wife was looking very upset.

'Oh, Gordon,' she said. 'I don't know how to ask this as I'm not really sure that I believe in what you do.'

'No, we don't believe in what you claim to do,' her husband interrupted. You had to see this man to believe him. He was so straight and serious I felt threatened by the sharp crease running down the front of his trousers. His hands were cleaner than a priest's. I felt as if I were standing in front of a headmaster.

'Please let me explain,' his wife went on. 'We cannot find a very expensive diamond bracelet.'

'No, *you* cannot find the bracelet, you stupid woman,' her husband interrupted.

'Look, what is it you expect me to do for you?' I chipped in.

'Well,' the lady pleaded, 'I have been told that you are psychic, although I don't know if we believe in that.'

'Oh, just get to the point, would you?' the husband squawked.

And all of this before the cup of coffee and cigarette that I normally need to get myself started each day!

The gist of the matter was that the lady had misplaced a very valuable bracelet that hadn't been insured and they wanted me to find it by means of psychic deduction.

'Let me ponder on this for a short while and I'll get back to you if I can be of any assistance,' I said. What I really meant was, 'Let me get the hell out of here and have a fag and a coffee!'

When I returned to the barbershop, I chuckled to myself about the ridiculous situation I found myself in. But even though it was laughable, I felt I had a duty to try and tune in and see if the spirit world would help the poor woman. After all, her husband seemed to be a difficult man. If I could assist in some way, she might be saved at least some of his recriminations.

'Come on, spirit friends,' I said, 'help a lady in need. After all, if this item of jewellery isn't found, she might end up as a message from *your* side!'

It was quite amazing. As soon as I closed my eyes, a man and woman were standing in front of me. They told me that they had bought the bracelet for their daughter's twenty-first birthday and then proceeded to show me where it was in the house of the warring couple.

I walked swiftly across the street to the newsagent's and relayed the following: 'You live in a white bungalow. As I walk through the front door, I can see before me three doors to my left and two doors to my right. The first door on my right is a bedroom. It is occupied by your mother-in-law.'

'That's quite correct,' said the astonished-looking lady.

'As I enter this room, I am aware of a cream-coloured carpet and bedroom furniture that matches. There is a window to my extreme right, where there sits a chest of five drawers. In the top drawer there is underwear. That is where your bracelet is.'

'That's amazing!'

'I hope I'm correct. But that's what I get,' I said.

I left the shop and returned to work. Within half an hour I had a phone call from the lady. She was in tears, telling me I was right. The missing object was in the top drawer of the chest of drawers.

At lunchtime, I walked into the shop to find the couple engaged in a shouting match.

'Well? Have you had him in our house or haven't you?' the husband was demanding.

'No, of course I haven't, dear.'

If the man were not so aggressive I would have laughed.

'You!' he screamed. 'How could you describe my home if you haven't been in it?'

There seemed to be no way to explain to him that the parents of his poor wife were anxious for her to find the bracelet so as not to have to face a scene much like the one she was presently enduring. Instead, I just asked for my cigarettes and said, 'Thanks would be nice!'

At the end of the day, however, the man did apologize and thank me kindly, even finishing with an offer of employment. A friend of his who worked for an oil company might offer me a position dowsing for oil. I wonder if you can guess what my answer was?

I am now 41. Already I would say I have experienced most folks' share of strange happenings. But by far the most unusual thing that I have ever experienced dates back to around 1991.

It was just after 6 p.m. one Sunday evening when the letterbox on my front door was rattled.

'Gordon, will you come over to see my dad?' Standing in front of me was a child, her face filled with excitement, panting breathlessly. 'Hurry, hurry!' she said. Her tiny hand pulled at mine with such urgency that I wasted no time asking questions but followed her across the street and up the stairs of the grey tenement building opposite. She was one of the children of a neighbouring family and her mother had been killed in a horrific road accident the previous week.

When we arrived at the front door of the second-floor flat, the child pushed it open and called out to her father, 'Da, he's here! Come on in, Gordon.'

In the sparsely furnished flat there were now five people – the two children, their father, the man who lived in the flat below and me. I was in the middle of enquiring about the urgency of the situation when the children's father stopped me.

'It's started again,' he said. As he uttered the words, loud rapping noises began to sound all around the living-room.

'You see,' he said to his downstairs neighbour. Apparently the neighbour had been complaining about the loud banging sounds that seemed to come from the flat above. They had started around midday and continued until that moment at intervals of around 20 minutes.

I had been asked to attend so-called 'haunted' houses before, but in most of the cases, sounds like the ones we were currently hearing could be explained as faulty central heating or movement in an old building. What made this phenomenon different was that there was an intelligent system of rapping that came in response to questions that were asked. It was rather like the experiences of the Fox sisters in Hydesville, America, in 1848. They had established communication with a murdered pedlar whose skeleton had been found some years later, and this led to the advent of modern Spiritualism. More than this, though, there was an intensity about this place that I had never experienced before. You could feel someone's presence in the very atmosphere.

What happened next took all of us by surprise. As we were standing around discussing the sounds coming from the walls and floor, the carpet lifted up, with everything on it – the three-piece suite, table, other furniture, three adult men and two children! This occurred several times in the course of about three minutes. It felt as if we were standing on some kind of surfboard, riding a wave.

A lot happened during the next ten minutes, but most was of a very personal nature and the only part that I can mention is that at all times there was a beautiful sense of peace and that we were given a most outstanding communication from the recently deceased lady. Such communications are intended only for those to whom they can bring love (and in this case hope) and who might understand the nature of the message.

I believe that the power of love can move many things on this Earth, whether or not that love comes from one living in this world or beyond the veil of death. Who am I to say? What I do know is that there really are many strange things between Heaven and Earth.

CHAPTER NINE

It has been my greatest joy to share my gift with those who most appreciate its worth. Among these are people from all walks of life, from the richest to the poorest, taking in many noted and renowned personalities. The one aspect they all have in common is that they have all suffered a deep loss at some point in their lives.

The difference between evidence from the spirit world that is said to be general and that considered to be excellent is the matter of unfinished business. I have experienced many cases of spirit contact where the deceased has passed to the Other Side in such an abrupt manner that they find themselves filled with a sense of urgency to contact their loved ones on the Earth plane. It is as if they have a need to console grieving relatives with the news of their survival.

Of the thousands of messages I have passed from the spirit world, most seem to confirm that no matter how a person dies, their spirit arrives on the Other Side intact and without having experienced the pains and torments that we on the Earth plane imagine they felt.

When someone who has died suddenly manages to come through to a loved one, they normally bring back a message of great significance. Can you imagine the look on a mother's face when her murdered child returns to tell her she has survived death and that she loves her – and then is able to back this up with information that only the grieving parent can understand? Or a woman whose husband went out to work in the morning and did not return to his wife in the evening? If he can pass to her words of comfort and guidance, she will be able to go on living instead of wasting away with grief. In cases like these, a medium's work is seen at its best.

Experiencing this type of sitting many times, I have come to realize the value of the work that the spirit world does for the bereaved, and feel honoured to be used by it. Being able to help people in this way is the motivation behind my mediumship. And if ever I do feel like giving up, the spirit world steps in.

One sitter the spirit world sent to me certainly reminded me about the reason for my work just at the point when I was about to give it all up… Those Above have impeccable timing. It was the end of

August 1997 and I was feeling exhausted with all of the work I had been doing, not to mention my nine-to-five at the barber's and two teenage sons to fit in somewhere. It was one of those moments when I felt I was spread so thinly that something had to give! I promised myself that after this sitting I would take a break and rebuild my energy, which was all but gone.

In the meantime, the caretaker of the Spiritualist church had set this sitting up for me and it was simply a case of waiting to see who would be the next sitter. Would this lady really need to have a sitting with a medium or would she be someone who wanted to know if she should get married, divorced or whatever?

When Mrs Bright eventually arrived, I knew instantly that she truly required help, although the look on her face said, 'What am I doing here?' It was clear to me she had not sat with a medium before, so I did my best to reassure her and the sitting got underway. I will allow her to describe to you what happened.

On 20 June 1997, my younger son Alan died in a road accident, just one month past his twenty-ninth birthday. Only someone who has suffered the same loss can come anywhere near understanding the devastating pain this caused us. As a mother, I felt I had let Alan down by not being able to prevent this from happening; I should have been able to protect him as I did when he was a child.

This is irrational, I know, but reason plays very little part in one's thinking at a time like this. The weeks following Alan's death passed in a mist of pain and anger – anger that such a fine young man should have been taken away from us in what seemed such a senseless way, anger with God for not protecting Alan, as I prayed each night He would protect my sons.

Pain enveloped us every waking moment, yet was still able to pierce you to the heart when you realized it was not a bad dream: the unthinkable really had happened. My husband Syd and I had lost a much-loved son; Iain had lost the brother he loved; Sarah had lost her husband of just three years.

Six weeks after Alan died, we were to go down to Hampshire for the interment of his ashes. At this point, I found life so difficult. I had a desperate need to know that Alan was safe, as silly as that may sound. I have always believed that physical death is not the end for us, but until now that had only been an emotional belief. Now I needed evidence of survival of the spirit.

I telephoned the Spiritualist church in Berkeley Street and asked if I could please arrange a private sitting with someone. It was my great good fortune that Jim, the caretaker, arranged for me to see Gordon Smith, and from that very first meeting I have felt blessed he was the person I saw.

Gordon was immediately able to make a link with Alan in such a way that I was in no doubt it was indeed him Gordon could hear. It was an unbelievably emotional sitting for me, but I came away from it with a serenity I would not have believed possible that morning when we set out. I still wept buckets, but could tell myself that Alan was safe; not only safe, but happy. This can be a difficult concept to accept, I know, as on the one hand of course I am glad that he is happy, and yet I miss him so dreadfully.

During the sitting with Gordon, he told me that two ladies had been with Alan after the accident and one had been holding his hand, which was exactly the case. He went on to describe the spare bedroom Alan used as a study, and said that Alan said I had moved the papers around, as indeed I had in order to find insurance and registration documents for the police.

Gordon also told me that Alan had been with me when I went through his wallet looking for his credit card as I had been asked to do. This was important to me because both Iain and Alan knew they could leave wallets or even letters or diaries lying around and I would not look at them. I have a great belief in one's right to privacy. I suppose a sceptic would say one could guess that naturally families would go through papers, etc, at such a time, and of course that is true. But no one could give by chance a detailed description of a room they have never seen.

At later sittings with Gordon, I had even more conclusive evidence that Alan's spirit still lived. There is absolutely no point in looking for earth-shattering pronouncements from 'the Other Side'. What on Earth would that prove? What I needed was personal proof it was indeed Alan who was channelling information to me through Gordon, and that is precisely what I received.

During one sitting, Gordon suddenly said that Alan had a very deep voice, as indeed he had. He said he had no idea why, but Alan was singing what sounded to him like a hymn, and then lah-lah-ed through the verse until he got to the last line, which was 'To be a pilgrim'. This made me laugh because Alan loathed this particular hymn. He'd had a thing about pilgrims since he was a little boy.

I was somewhat surprised when Gordon told me that Alan was showing him the bathroom, the layout of which he accurately described, but then said we would come back to it. We carried on with the sitting, but eventually Gordon said he had to come back to the bathroom, but he was not quite sure how to interpret what Alan was telling him.

Very quickly Gordon had built up a good link with Alan and was able to tell me that Alan was laughing, so he was not quite sure what he was letting himself in for. The reason he was reluctant to come back to the bathroom was that Alan had told him there was a bird in there. Of course, people do not normally keep birds in the bathroom. I was stunned when I heard this because I knew exactly what Alan meant.

When we bought this house, we all had a laugh at the bathroom because the previous owners put a transfer on the underside of the loo seat's lid. The transfer was of a large winking owl! Hardly a common bathroom decoration and certainly not something anyone could guess. This really hit the mark because when we finally replaced the bathroom suite, Alan complained so much about the missing owl that I bought a small bronze owl to sit in the bathroom.

I was longing to tell Iain all about my time with Gordon, but since he was going off on a course, I knew I would have to tell him by telephone. However, we had promised to call in to see his wife Sam and his daughter Bryony on the way home, as Sam was also anxious to hear about it.

One thing Gordon said puzzled me. He said that Alan was showing him a doorbell and I simply could not think what this signified. Gordon said not to worry about it and just keep it in mind.

Imagine my surprise when we were leaving Iain and Sam's house to see a doorbell, where before there had been just two wires showing since the door had been replaced some weeks previously. I asked Sam when Iain had fixed the bell. She told me he had done it on the Friday night, the night before I saw Gordon. Not only could Gordon not have known this, but I did not know it had been done, which rather rules out telepathy, suggestion or anything of that sort.

As I said earlier, it is the evidence of a shared history that gives the best possible proof of survival of the spirit. This incident of the doorbell may seem trivial, but it was so important to us, and in particular to Iain, who wanted very much to believe and who was so close to Alan that Alan would know he needed proof.

Each time I had a sitting with Gordon, I left feeling that I had spent time in Alan's company – it was just that I could not see him or hug him. The evidence Gordon has been able to give me has been outstanding. I have only been able to give a very few instances of it here. There have been no generalizations. It has all been relevant to us. In fact, it has not only helped me, of course, but I have also been able to pass evidence on to my husband, to Iain and to Sarah.

The effects have been felt even outside the family. I was able to contact the young lady who had held Alan's hand after the accident and tell her that he was aware of her being there. She was so glad to know this, as she had been undergoing therapy since the accident. Knowing she had helped Alan helped her. So the love Alan was sending to us allowed me to extend it to her too.

Although there were many pieces of evidence I was able to pass on to Iain, I knew he would want to come with me to see Gordon at some point. It was exactly one year from the date of the accident that he did this.

We had a splendid sitting, with much of the evidence being directed toward Iain, who was both moved and gratified to hear Gordon repeat Alan's words. I felt right from the first time I had a sitting with Gordon that Alan trusted him, had a rapport with him and on several occasions took great pleasure in 'winding him up'. The day Iain came with me was one such occasion.

Having assured Iain on the way to Glasgow that there would be nothing 'spooky' about the whole thing, we arrived in Berkeley Street. As we drove along looking for somewhere to park, he asked which house it was and I had to tell him it was the one with white sheets draped over the railings! The church was being decorated. Then we went downstairs to the sitting room, which I was amazed to find was almost in darkness. This was quite the opposite of how the room usually looked in the early afternoon.

When I spoke to Gordon later he had no idea why he had drawn the curtains on this particular day. He had simply felt that he must. I am sure Alan found it highly amusing to watch Iain's reaction to the scene he found. It did not put him off, however, and he soon felt as strongly as I did that Alan was with us. In fact, when we came out he gave me a hug and said, 'Mum, we've been talking to Alan.'

The evidence Gordon gave Iain that day had a great effect on him. He was hurting so badly at the loss of the brother he was so close to and with whom he had shared so much. Through the generous sharing of his outstanding gifts as a medium, Gordon has made it possible for us as a family to go on. He has shown us beyond the shadow of a doubt that our spirit does live on and that Alan will always be with us.

It is a rule of mine never to give more than two private sittings to any one person. In the case of Lee Bright, it was more to do with her son on the Other Side. Alan had assured me that his mother required an extra sitting and he was sure his brother would be brought along. The look on his brother's face when he realized Alan was communicating really was a picture.

Alan was what I call a good communicator. He was so eager to communicate when he got the chance that he was going to make the best of it. He has given his mother so much evidence that I cannot even begin to remember it all. One thing that sticks in my mind happened on the second sitting I did for his mother. Lee had just entered my house when I heard Alan's voice clearly call out to me, 'Ask Mum about *Macbeth*.' Instead of greeting Lee with 'Hello', I said, 'What about *Macbeth*?' Her eyes widened with surprise. 'I've only just bought a copy of the play on the way here this morning,' she said.

In the year or so that I have known Lee Bright, I've witnessed a great change in her. To see such a positive change in a person and know that in some way you have contributed is truly wonderful. The effect of this sitting on me was also quite amazing. Instead of the fatigue I had been feeling at the outset, I felt as though I had been given a great boost of energy. All of the clouds of doubt lifted from my mind and I felt privileged to be able to help someone through a very deep emotional experience such as this. It's this type of reward that all mediums feel when their gift has been used correctly.

Here are two further statements from people who have sought help from me. The first is from Malcolm Bryce, who contacted me after the death of his brother.

I first saw Gordon some five weeks after I lost my brother in rather sad circumstances. He'd had a very short illness and was only in early middle age. A great friend who knew Gordon was concerned for me because of my reaction to the death. The air was not clear. Things were left unsaid. Two sides of a situation remained unresolved. I was in distress.

My friend spoke to Gordon and asked him if he would give me a private sitting. Busy as he was, he agreed to do so. I had never met him or seen him demonstrate before. A date was set for the following Tuesday, and that was the first I knew of the arrangement.

However, on the Sunday afternoon I was feeling very low and decided to go to the Spiritualist church in Somerset Place for the evening service. It was a last minute thought. I arrived just in time and sat near the door.

It was announced that the medium booked to appear was not able to be there and Gordon Smith would speak and give the demonstration. He had been called in at the last minute.

It was a warm and friendly meeting. I was intrigued to watch Gordon, who was to give me a sitting within a few days. Toward the end of the demonstration, he was giving information to an elderly lady near the front. Then, quite out of context of the message, he asked her if she liked music: he was surrounded by music, my brother's passion and his profession. She accepted the message.

Could she take the number 18? This was my brother's birthdate, which was only a week or so away. She would think about it. I was convinced the message was for me, but felt I could not butt in. Gordon spoke so distinctively again about the music. I was excited inside.

'Wednesday is significant,' he said, looking to the lady. Again, she gave a vague reply. On the previous Saturday evening a dear friend had phoned to tell me her husband had passed away peacefully. That was also a reason for me being very low and sensitive on the Sunday. His funeral was to be on Wednesday.

I felt that Gordon was not convinced these remarks were for this lady, but he carried on, then started a new message for someone else. I felt my brother had been there even if I had not acknowledged it publicly. I left the service as soon as it finished.

On the Tuesday evening, I made my way to my friend's house and was introduced to Gordon. We chatted briefly, but I made no mention of my Sunday visit until after the sitting. We sat together and fell into silence.

Gordon then spoke of hearing music and being surrounded by lights, not spiritual lights but flashing, colourful disco-type lights. I felt my brother was there as all this was very significant. 'He is with a lady with the initial "A",' said Gordon. Our mother's initial. 'I'm being given the number 18.' My brother's birthdate, which had come through on the Sunday.

'He's telling me "Wednesday".' I told Gordon about my going to the funeral the next day. 'No, that's not it,' and after a few moments Gordon said, 'He's telling me Wednesday was the night you all spent with him before he passed.' Indeed, it was an all-night vigil. It confirmed to me that I was not wrong in my feelings on the Sunday, and what good evidence this was, not only repeated, but explained.

Gordon continued to give me in total 12 detailed pieces of information as proof of my brother's presence. These included a nickname; a significant reference to my sister; that I was going on holiday soon; that it would be really good for me to get away for a change of scene after the bereavement; and that I was leaving in another week or so.

There was no specific mention of the unresolved matters, but the evidence and warmth of feeling coming through gave me great comfort. I felt there was an understanding that helped me to reconcile myself to the situation, to my extreme relief.

Since then I have seen Gordon demonstrate several times and had evidential messages from Spirit through him. On one occasion, Gordon was giving quite a specific message to a young woman. He then said that someone from Spirit was impatient and wanting to get through. It sounded like my brother, as everyone's timing had to suit him!

Gordon told the spirit contact to wait and continued his message. Within 20 seconds or so, he apologized and said that this spirit person was so impatient he had to interrupt. I said to my companion, 'That's my brother,' and so it was. His personality came through before the message itself.

On two other occasions from the platform Gordon asked if someone could accept a piece of information, a small but significant detail about a ring. I could, and each time the messages that followed were indeed for me.

What was remarkable was that the initial linking of such small detail was exactly the same each time and the two demonstrations were at least a year apart. I value Gordon as a wonderful medium and now as a friend.

The next statement comes from a fellow medium, Mary Armour, whose work is highly respected. It just goes to show that even mediums find it difficult to tune in when it comes to themselves.

I first met Gordon one evening when I was serving the Jean Primrose church in Glasgow. I was invited by Mrs Primrose to stay behind after the service and sit in her development circle. It became apparent to me on that night that Gordon had a gift far greater than any other in the circle. When I came home, I sent him a little card wishing him well and thanking him for the remarkable message he had given to me.

Over the years I have watched this young man of great ability grow from a fledgling into a spiritual dove. In my opinion, he is among the greatest in the world.

Now for some of the remarkable evidence and spirit forecasts through the mediumship of Gordon Smith.

I have been fortunate to have three trance sittings with Gordon. He is, in my opinion, one of the few who at this time is a channel for the great materialization medium Helen Duncan.

The first sitting when Helen came through concerned evidence about my father. It was known only to me.

At the second sitting, on 27 January 1997, Helen came through and said, 'Mary, please be careful about your ankle.' On 14 February I fell and fractured my ankle.

In a more recent sitting, in September 1998, he gave me a message from Helen containing information that I know to be true but, as Spirit says, the best evidence is that for which you have to search.

On the same night, Dominica, his guide, talked about a lady, Mrs Jean Simes. I said I was sorry, but I did not know her. But on returning home, my mother asked about the sitting. I said I could not understand the last evidence received concerning Jean Simes.

'How do you know that?' my mother asked. 'She died on Friday.' Her friend Mary had told her about it the previous day. My mother was quite taken aback.

I wish Gordon well. As an ambassador for Spirit, the world could find no better.

CHAPTER TEN

'What's it like on the Other Side?' 'Is there really life after physical death?' Questions like these are put to me all the time. I guess most people are looking for some form of solid evidence that will quell their fears of dying.

There *is* life after death. Of that I am certain. I have had so much evidence of survival that I can no longer say I just *believe* in the hereafter, I *know* that life goes on after death. And there is an enormous difference between believing and knowing.

As for the question of what it's like on the Other Side, that's just a little bit more difficult to answer. Many books have been written by people claiming to have journeyed to the spirit world, most of them describing beautiful countryside with flowers and birds whose colours are beyond description. It has been said there are great halls of learning and hospitals where new arrivals can rest and recuperate. Stories are told of evolved assessors dressed in long white robes, whose role it is to help you understand the life you have just lived. There are descriptions of houses, cottages and grand cities that surpass any in this world.

There are so many different reports and descriptions of the life to come that it is difficult to believe any of them. It is my understanding that each individual description is relevant only to the person who experiences it. Each mind will gravitate to a level of understanding most suited to its concept of Heaven, as it were. It would seem that on the Other Side our minds progressively move away from material ideas. It is a bit like a snake shedding its skins as it goes through life. Once again, it reminds me of my spiritual development here and now, and how the most valuable lesson I learned was to *un*learn and carry much less mental baggage.

I have had several personal experiences of the Hereafter. Each particular encounter has been incredible and although I have never registered anything of a physical nature, at all times I have been in contact with the consciousness of different spirit people. The best way I can describe these encounters is to say that after each one I was left feeling more vital than ever before. It is the most difficult thing to explain, for there are no words to adequately portray the images that you sense during these amazing journeys. The feelings of life and light are most predominant. On each occasion, I remember being aware of a strong pulsing, like a heart beat. But this rhythmic sensation seemed to be in harmony with all of the different sensations of life that were present. There were times when I thought I was seeing someone I knew, but the sense of sight was so much more intense and went beyond the visual sense that I am used to. It was the same with words, though at no point did I ever speak to anyone. Everything that was communicated was done by thought. More than that, on some occasions it was a communication of feelings.

One such spiritual encounter I shall never forget happened on 15 May 1994. I had just come home from a hard day's work at the barbershop and I decided to have a nap before my evening meal. I lay on the settee and all sorts of trivial thoughts were passing through my mind when a vision of a man aged about 30 flashed before me.

I became aware of my entire body gently vibrating, almost as if the couch I lay on was swaying. At the same time, my mind began to focus more intensely on the young man, who seemed to be familiar to me yet had something about his appearance that I couldn't recognize.

There was a feeling so compelling about this man that I seemed to be drawn toward him. I knew what it was like to experience an out-of-body state, but this was different. I felt as if I were travelling and yet was very aware of my body lying quite lifeless on the settee.

Then I felt a sharp pull around my solar plexus and I was moving at high speed toward a light about the size of a pinhead. The whole episode felt like the sudden sensation you get on the steepest drop of a roller-coaster when it rushes toward the ground at high speed. All at once the rush was over. I had no sensation of my physical body.

The man who had drawn me to this state of altered reality was still with me. At first he appeared to be in his early thirties, but when I was spiralled to his realm of spirit reality, I suddenly sensed him as a child of ten or thereabouts. It was my cousin Stephen, who had died almost 20 years earlier.

Stephen took me on a journey through a realm of spiritual beauty which I cannot relay in words. All I know is that I was in a state of grace. From this point, I could understand life, love and beauty in a way I had never known before. What I felt in this state was completely electric. As long as I live, I will never forget it.

The last I recalled of Stephen was the sound of his voice just as I was about to wake from this state. I remember it the way most people recollect their waking dreams as they emerge from sleep in the morning. Stephen was standing in front of me, smiling. Then he said, 'I'll be with my mother on 22 June.' At this, I awoke with a start.

I couldn't fully take in what had happened, but the closing message stayed with me for the rest of the evening. I wondered if I should phone his mother and tell her, but then thought better of it, as it might disturb her. Instead, I wrote down the date Steve had given me so that at some point I could ask his mum if it meant anything to her.

When I eventually got round to speaking to my Aunt Sylvia, I mentioned the date, but she assured me that it meant nothing to her. After this, I thought no more about it. I supposed it could have been a mistake or maybe I had misunderstood what was actually said.

It must have been near the end of the same year when I next saw Aunt Sylvia, during one of my visits to London. When I walked into her home, I was completely shocked to see this once very beautiful lady looking more like a victim of a prisoner-of-war camp.

Sylvia couldn't help but notice the look of horror on my face and explained that she had been fighting stomach cancer for almost five years; She was now at a stage where nothing more could be done for her and it appeared that she had only a short time left on the Earth plane.

For the next couple of months, I kept in constant contact with my aunt. I hoped to hear that by some miracle or other the doctors had made a mistake and that she wasn't as ill as they claimed, or perhaps an operation might give her a fighting chance. But all the hoping and praying I did were to no avail.

I was distraught that the woman I thought of as a second mother should have to face the same fate as her beloved son. After Stephen's death Aunt Sylvia had changed her career, giving up a successful job in London to train as a nurse. After qualifying, she went on to work as a Macmillan Nurse, serving patients suffering from cancer. What sad irony life can sometimes throw at us.

On Saturday 17 June 1995, I decided to fly down to London, as I felt it would be my last chance to see Sylvia, who had booked herself into a hospice for her remaining days. Before I left Glasgow, I bought two red roses. I put one into a vase at home and took the other to London to give to Sylvia.

When I arrived at her room in a very pleasant building set in beautiful grounds, I saw my aunt sitting with soaking wet hair, waiting for me to cut and blow dry it! She said, 'Gordon, I want to look my best when I meet Stephen.' She was very strong about the whole thing. In fact, she refused to accept any form of pain relief, saying that when she passed on she wanted to be of a very clear mind.

She explained she had been with her son on several occasions and that he had told her that he would be waiting for her to begin her new journey on the Other Side with him. Many people would say that a person in the last stages of a cancerous illness would be hallucinating when claiming to talk to the so-called 'dead', and I might be inclined to agree with them in some cases, but not in this one. Sylvia was the most level-headed woman anyone could ever meet. Even now, she was able to arrange her funeral service as well as her own personal business. Not only that, but all the members of staff who had looked after her in the hospice were called to her bedside one at a time, given an envelope and thanked for their care and attention. No matter how ill she was, Sylvia was still very sober-minded.

When I decided to leave later that day, Sylvia asked me to come closer to her. By this time she looked very tired.

'Darling,' she said. 'I am about to take a step on a new journey. I am not afraid. Please don't cry for me. Think of me being reunited with my dear son.'

How could I cry for such a brave lady? As I was about to leave, I turned to her and said, 'I'll see you around some time.'

At this, she smiled broadly at me and retorted, 'Well, if anyone does, I suppose you will, kid.'

On returning to Glasgow later that evening, the first thing I noticed when I entered my house was the rose. It appeared to be dead, but even so I was reluctant to throw it out. I just stood and gazed at this once beautiful flower, now wilting. I couldn't help but compare it to the beautiful English rose I had just left in the same condition a few hours earlier.

On the evening of Wednesday 21 June, I went to bed and prayed the same prayer that I had been praying for the last week or so – that God would allow Sylvia gracious passage into the spirit world.

The following morning, I awoke suddenly to sit bolt upright in my bed. I immediately looked at my watch. It was 5 a.m. I could hear a familiar voice by my left ear saying, 'See you around, darling.' It was Sylvia. She had gone … and on the very date her son had given to me two years previously.

I waited until 8 a.m. to call my Uncle Michael in London, to be told what I already knew: 'Sylvia died at 5 o'clock this morning.' I have often wondered how those in the spirit world know of such events so far in advance.

Later that morning, I noticed that the rose in my living-room had come back to life. It was in full bloom and continued like this for a further ten days. My uncle said later that the rose I gave to Sylvia seemed to die at the very same time as she let go of this world.

This was a strange episode for me and yet just one of many I have experienced relating to life after death. I suppose that the most evidential experiences of the afterlife are indeed on a personal level. Albert Best, who also had many encounters with the spirit world, would say, 'Other than those who experienced it, who would believe it?' And, of course, he was right.

As I said earlier, each person who finds themselves in the spirit world seems to relate to different sorts of material things that can be found there. On the evidence given, it is my opinion that we create our own kingdom come, that each of us arrives at a place where we will find comfort and beauty according to the state of our own mind when departing from this world. With this in mind, I try to be careful of how I live my life on the Earth plane. This is not out of fear of retribution on the Other Side, but more out of a desire to gravitate to a state of beauty there.

There *is* life after death, of this I am sure. But the important aspect to take from this knowledge is that the people who are left behind in this world must learn to go on with their lives after the death of a loved one.

And if you have created a bond of love with another in this world, then nothing – not even death – can separate you from them.

CHAPTER ELEVEN

Prove It!

No matter how many times a medium provides sound evidence of life after death, there will always be those who insist that there are other, more logical explanations than the survival of the human spirit. Yet as long ago as the 1850s, mediums like Daniel Dunglas Home permitted some of the most eminent scientists of the day to investigate their highly controversial mediumistic abilities. Like all mediums who know their gift is genuine and inspired only by a higher spiritual source, these early pioneers willingly offered scientists the chance to attend some of the most famous seances in the history of Spiritualism.

I mention D. D. Home because in all the years he practised his rare brand of mediumship, he was never found to be fraudulent. Nor were his seances conducted in the dark. This Scots-born natural medium produced great feats of levitation and materialization in well-lit rooms in full view of many learned and professional men. All in all, he was probably one of the greatest exponents of mediumship known to humanity. Furthermore, he never charged for his gifts, yet another true mark of true spiritual mediumship. Amongst his countless sitters were the then Czar of Russia and the German Kaiser.

Within the last 150 years, mediums such as D. D. Home, Leonore Piper, the Bangs sisters, Helen Duncan, Helen Hughes, Ena Twigg, Leslie Flint, Albert Best and many more have worked so hard to prove that there is life after death. All of them brought comfort and inspiration to many people as well as perhaps helping science discover a little more about the nature of the human spirit. And each of these mediums showed great trust in the gifts they were given by God.

In 1994, I was asked by Tricia Robertson, of the Scottish Society for Psychical Research, if I would give a demonstration of mediumship at Glasgow University for society members and the public. The event was to be hosted by Professor Archie Roy, Emeritus Professor of Astronomy at Glasgow University. I agreed without giving the matter much thought.

It is strange how I don't perceive something as a challenge when it lies in the distant future, only to find as the time draws nearer that I wish I'd never opened my big mouth! It's at times like these that I am bombarded by negative thoughts about how it could all go wrong. What if nothing happens on the night? What if no one can understand any of the messages that come through? So many times I've put myself and my mediumship out on that limb. I have faced the same fears time and time again, whether before working at the university, or in a theatre in Gibraltar, or even in some of the large halls I have demonstrated in up and down the United Kingdom. And the more I think about the outcome of such events, the more I end up a nervous wreck.

This is where the term 'nil by mind' always comes back to me. At the end of the day, if there is to be contact with the Other Side, and if it is to be seen as good or otherwise, should not really affect me beforehand. Neither I nor anyone else will ever change future events by worrying about them.

So here I was once again standing in a large hall filled to capacity, only this time most of the audience, whom I would insist on calling a con-gregation, were there to investigate my work on a scientific level rather than out of need or in search of spiritual fulfilment.

All I remember of that night is Professor Roy's marvellous introduction of me. After that, I just said to the spirit people, 'Come on, please don't let me down!' Of course, they did not.

Following the demonstration, I was invited to

answer questions from members of the audience. Most of them came from academic backgrounds. By that time, of course, I had given a successful display of mediumship. Besides, all I had to do was answer truthfully. So I was full of confidence!

Since that first night, I have been asked back to the university several times. On one of these occasions the strangest thing happened. It was my third visit and I had been asked to take questions before the clairvoyance. A gentleman sitting in the front row asked me, 'Gordon, isn't it true that all a medium does is read body language accompanied by telepathic information that they pick up from the recipient's brain?'

'No, sir,' I said. 'For one thing, there have been many occasions where mediums – including me – have given evidence to people that they knew nothing about. Then there are other incidences when the medium has provided information about something in that particular person's family which was taking place at that very moment and the recipient was unaware of it. There are volumes of records held within the archives of the Society for Psychical Research in London with sworn statements to back up what I say.'

However, the man didn't have to check the archives. The spirit world decided to prove the very point that night. I had not long begun the demonstration – in fact, it was the second communication of the night – when I became aware of a spirit lady standing beside me. She told me her name was Anne and that her son was at the back.

Mentally, I asked her, 'How long ago did you pass?'

'Last week,' came the reply.

Oh dear, I thought. *There is someone up there who has just lost their dear mother.* I was sure they would still be grieving terribly.

'Is there a man at the back of the hall whose mother Anne has recently passed over?' I asked.

Silence.

Come on, Anne, I said in my mind. *Give me something else.*

'He is wearing my ring on the chain around his neck,' she whispered.

'Is there a gentleman who would be wearing his mother's ring on a chain around his neck?' I asked.

Again, complete silence.

Right, Anne, I'll give you one more try, I thought. *Tell me where you lived.*

'Maryhill Road,' was her instant reply.

Still nothing.

'OK,' I said. 'If no one can understand this, then I must move on to the next message.'

Just as I went to walk across to the other side of the podium, a voice in my ear said, 'There he is.' As I looked back to the furthest point of the large hall, there was a man's face looking through one of the glass partitions in the door. He was one of the university janitors trying to have a peek at what was going on.

'That's Jim,' the voice said. 'That's my boy!'

'Please could you come in?' I called to the unsuspecting man, waving him into the room with my hand. I'm sure he thought I was mad. Everyone in the hall turned to see this rather embarrassed man in his forties standing there in his long tan-coloured attendant's coat.

'Is your name Jim?' I called out. This was a do-or-die situation for me. If this wasn't the son of my spirit lady, then I'd better give up.

'Yes,' the man said in a quiet voice. He really must have been wondering what was going on!

'Please do excuse me, Jim. But are you wearing a chain around your neck?'

'Yes.' By now he appeared to be baffled by the proceedings.

'Is there a ring on that chain that would have belonged to your mother?'

As I was finishing the question, Jim was in the process of producing the two items of jewellery for all to see.

'Your mother's name – was it Anne?' I quickly continued.

Suddenly, the man looked very emotional. He nodded his head in agreement.

'Finally, Maryhill Road. Does that mean anything to you, sir?'

'My mother lived there,' he said, looking completely astonished.

Once the information had been accepted, Anne went on to give the most incredibly detailed message to her son, all of it personal to him alone. It seemed he was there quite by chance, as he had taken a wrong turning in one of the corridors and found himself outside that particular lecture theatre wondering what was taking place that evening.

Once I had delivered the message, I thanked Jim for taking the wrong turning and making my message understood, and turned my attention to the gentleman who had raised the point about body language and telepathy.

'Sir,' I said, 'I do hope this contact from the Other Side will answer your question. After all, I am sure you will agree that in order to read someone's body language that person must be in front of you. As for telepathy, I think the person involved would have to be sending out telepathic messages in order that I, the would-be receiver in this case, might pick them up. Even so, it would seem unlikely that this man was even aware of any such practices taking place around him.'

It is cases like this one that highlight spiritual mediumship in such a way that even the most sceptical of people would have to agree there is *something* going on around us that is greater than we can conceive. Even some of the most learned men of science have had to accept that not everything has a perfectly logical explanation. Nor indeed does the world of science hold the key that will eventually open up the doors to some of the greatest mysteries known to humanity. But maybe if people from all areas of life who wish to unveil these mysteries work together, then there is a chance that the information will start to present itself.

Psychical research groups have been trying for decades to uncover some of this information. As mentioned earlier, some of these organizations and societies have on file sworn affidavits by many eminent figures throughout the years concerning case upon case of psychic and spiritual phenomena that have happened before their very eyes. Some of these phenomena still await an explanation.

As a medium, I believe it is my duty to assist these people as much as I am able. If my contribution to science has even fractionally advanced our understanding of spiritual matters, at least I will have offered something. It is far better to have tried than to have died of ignorance, which to me is the way of those who will not even look at a subject for fear of change. So I have allowed my mediumship to be subjected to experiments in the hope that knowledge will grow from them. I have assisted true seekers in tests, blind tests and double-blind tests. It doesn't matter to me whether people believe what I do is genuine. All I can say is that I try my best.

It is nice to know that there are serious-minded people who support mediumship, but those who don't understand it and who haven't even bothered to learn what it is really about have no right to form opinions about its causes and effects.

Professor Archie Roy became convinced of the powers of true mediumship after having a private sitting with my dear friend Albert Best. He speaks openly of this in his book *A Sense of Something Strange*. Since then, he has become a great modern-day pioneer in trying to prove there is life after death.

Both Professor Roy and Tricia Robertson are, among others, trying to establish a scientific approach to studying the evidence given by mediums to their recipients in order to dispel the age-old claim that the information given is no more than general. The following is an account by Tricia Robertson from her book *The Truth is in Here*.

PRISM is an acronym for Psychical Research Involving Selected Mediums. This is a research group that was set up to study para-normal phenomena, including mediumship, in a scientific manner.

One of the criticisms of mediums made by sceptics is the hypothesis that mediums' statements are so general that they could apply to anyone. Under the auspices of PRISM, this hypothesis is being experimentally tested using statistical mathematical methods.

The first phase of experimentation has used a large number of statistics, having been carried out over a period of two years or so. Using the first phase protocol, the results showed that mediums' statements to recipients were indeed meaningful. The odds against the results being due to chance are ten thousand million to one.

Gordon Smith was one of the mediums who willingly participated in this first phase. The statistical analysis of his results always showed a high degree of accuracy to the intended recipient.

It was because of the high standard of his work that he was asked to give a demonstration of his mediumship at Glasgow University at the request of the Scottish Society for Psychical Research. No one was disappointed.

So how does it work? If I had a penny for every time someone asked me that, I'd be a very rich man! It would be all too easy to say 'I am clairvoyant' or 'clairaudient' or even 'clairsentient', meaning that I 'see', 'hear' and 'sense' the so-called 'dead', but the fact is that my mediumship works differently each time and there are times when these three aspects work simultaneously. I am certain that all mediums are aware of this.

When I was a child, I simply accepted my mediumistic gifts as part of my nature. To hear spirit voices was as natural to me as hearing those of my parents and other members of the family. To see visions concerning the future or to sense deep emotions from other people was also quite common for me. Looking back, I can see that when other people questioned what I was doing, it put doubts in my mind about what I was really experiencing. As with any natural gifts, left to themselves, psychic abilities will develop in the proper way, but if we try to dissect them, we actually block their flow.

After watching the progression of the many aspects of mediumship I have had in my life, though, I find I now have a much clearer understanding of how it works. Each private sitting or message at a public demonstration is completely different. Sometimes I 'hear' the spirit people. Usually this happens when the spirit visitor was a very good communicator on this side. They will still be adept on the Other Side, as we take all our skills – good and bad! – with us.

On other occasions, I might 'sense' a spirit communicator, yet 'see' and 'hear' nothing. Again, I feel this is due to the personality of the spirit contact. When just 'sensing', all I can do is to describe the feelings they emanate. After all, not everyone likes to say exactly what they are thinking, which is probably just as well sometimes! Those I 'sense' may well be remembered for their quiet personalities.

As for 'seeing' spirit personalities, this often accompanies clairaudience or clairsentience. As I said, sometimes all three work simultaneously.

What some people don't fully appreciate is that not only does the spirit person's personality affect the communication, but the conditions of both the medium and recipient add or take away from the contact. If I am not feeling 100 per cent, messages from the Other Side may well be distorted to a greater or lesser extent. This happens if I am feeling exceptionally tired or stressed. It is a bit like a radio running on a weak battery.

Sitters also play an important role. If they put up barriers or arrive in a very sceptical state and are sitting there tight-lipped and frowning with their arms folded, I am more inclined to be put off. Those who seek help should at least arrive open-minded.

Each and every sitting ought to be regarded as something of an experiment in which the medium aims to merge the two worlds to prove that loved ones have survived and that they have retained their intelligence, memory, personality and individuality.

Communicators return because of ties of love and affection. No one can 'call up' the so-called 'dead' There is a reason for this. If mediums could dial up anyone at the drop of a hat, some dictator would soon be trying to contact Hitler or Stalin!

At the end of the day, my mediumship works best when there is a need for it to do so. I feel that the spirit world responds to those who are hurting. It is like a heightened sense that switches on in response to emotional pain in the same way that animals react when becoming aware of danger.

Be that as it may, I always seem to answer the question of how my mediumship works with another question: why does it work?

CHAPTER TWELVE

Mediumship

'What's that thing called you do, Gordon, that religious thing, you know whit ah mean?'

My mother still cannot understand what I demonstrate at weekends. She normally tells people that I do something religious, but she isn't too sure what it involves. I find that quite funny, although to be fair to my mum she's the first to say she's proud of me, even if she doesn't know why!

Some people think of me as a very spiritual person. If there is a spirituality there that others recognize, it is mostly inherited from my parents. I have already mentioned how naturally kind they both are. But more than this, it is all their wonderful traits and attributes and eccentricities that have bred in me the ability to laugh through some of the most difficult times in my life.

I remember visiting my parents shortly after

Dad underwent an operation to replace both his damaged kneecaps with plastic ones. After asking him how he was managing, I turned to Mum and said, 'He's doing quite well, isn't he?' She replied, with her usual deadpan expression, 'Well, if you really want to know what ah think, ah think that wee man is trying to escape from me bit by bit and he's gettin' rebuilt somewhere else!'

Then she looked at Dad and said, 'Sammy, don't sit too near that fire. They plastic knees o' yours might melt.' My dad just shook his head and sighed.

Between the two of them they could supply some great material for a comedy. But through every storm they have endured in their lives they've held each other together and they've helped many other people through hard times as well. I don't think I would have learned any more spiritual lessons if I'd been brought up by Mother Teresa and Gandhi – though the house would probably have been a lot quieter!

Isn't it strange that just when you think you know where your life is going, just when you think you know who you are and what you want to achieve, you are turned in a completely different direction? I always believed I would open up my own hair-dressing salon and be highly successful, then settle down in a nice house in the suburbs and enjoy all the trappings of success. But it's not quite that simple when you wake up one morning with spirit people standing at the foot of your bed reminding you, 'Hey, you're a medium, so you'd better forget all that and get on with it.'

Having lived that very ordinary life then followed the spiritual pathway, I must say, though, that the latter is much more fulfilling. Working as a medium for over a third of my life now, I've been very fortunate, if not to say very well guided. I've been blessed with good, sensible teachers and friends who have become like family. I've been taught how to become myself in such a short space of time. I've developed self-awareness, mindfulness and self-confidence that have changed my understanding of life entirely. Becoming a medium has brought many beautiful changes to my life. If I ever feel down, I can never be despondent for very long. Almost every day I see someone who is suffering the deep emotional pain that bereavement brings. That is a reminder that my life isn't so bad after all.

A medium's soul is much like that of an artist or musician. When you are in the flow of your craft, everything about you comes to life. There is a wonderful sense of magic about you and what you do. It feels as if you are creating beauty in the form of healing souls whose hearts have been broken in two.

The life of the medium is like the movement of waves: one moment you experience such highs and the next you drop to the depths of emptiness because of the withdrawal of that high energy.

I once compared my work as a medium to that of a piano. Imagine a great master playing to an audience of hundreds. Every note he strikes touches the hearts of people in such a way as to inspire passion. But when the concert is over, the piano is once more an inanimate object, just an instrument empty of sound. It is the same with a medium. There is no great admiration for what you are, only for what you can do. But being able to share that gift with those who are in emotional pain and allowed to witness the healing that takes place because of it is my greatest reward.

CHAPTER THIRTEEN

Whenever I am asked to sum up the meaning of spirituality, I find it very difficult. What I understand to be spiritual may not be seen that way by another. The fact that you practise a religion does not necessarily make you spiritual, although I am certain that spirituality can be found in all the world's religions if you are sincere in your quest.

Since the day I first walked through the doors of a Spiritualist church, I have found that my mental capacity has expanded so much that I now feel like a completely different person. No matter how I try to explain this, even in the simplest terms, I still cannot find a better description than the words that were written more than 50 years ago by the Reverend John Lamont, BD, a close friend of Sir Arthur Conan Doyle. As well as writing the world-famous Sherlock Holmes stories, Sir Arthur was a convinced and dedicated Spiritualist. He proclaimed Spiritualism's message from public platforms not only in the United Kingdom but also abroad and wrote several books on the subject, some of which are still in print, though sadly less well known than those about his fictional detective. The Rev. Lamont told Sir Arthur:

> *Spiritualism has been to me, in common with many others, such a lifting of the mental horizons and letting in of the heavens that I can only compare it to sailing on board ship, living as a prisoner below deck with all hatches battened down, then suddenly one night being allowed on deck for the first time, to the stupendous mechanism of the heavens all aglow with the glory of God.*

I would have to agree. That is how it felt for me.

As I remember, there were no religious pictures of holy statues in our family home. Neither was there any pressure on us to attend church on a Sunday. Religion was not a major part of my early life. In fact, even in school religious education just amounted to a quick skim through the Bible, as most state schools in those days taught only the Christian doctrine. Eastern religions, like Buddhism, Hinduism and so on, were completely denied to us.

Now I find that I am intrigued by most of the world's religions and philosophies. In all of these great teachings I can see that the most important feature is the need to promote spiritual awareness. It is my understanding that all the true religions are connected by the same golden thread of spirituality, which one day may unite them all. It doesn't matter which road you travel to seek your God, for all roads eventually lead to Heaven.

When I set out to discover more about spirituality, I began by reading as many spiritual works as I could. But reading books could only satisfy a part of my expanding consciousness, so whenever I found a lecture or discussion group on any religious subject I took myself along, hoping to absorb as much knowledge as my sponge-like mind would allow.

Then I decided to try a different approach. I did what most spiritual junkies do. I looked for a new fix – a meditation class.

In the western world, meditation is sometimes taught by people who wouldn't know spiritual enlightenment if it dropped on their head. On one occasion, I attended a so-called 'spiritual seminar' run by someone who claimed to have become enlightened after spending a couple of weeks in an ashram in India. I am sure he recouped most of his airfare that day alone, charging us £25 each.

I listened to so much nonsense in the quest to further my spiritual knowledge that I began to realize the only thing that was developing in me was a deep cynicism about some of the ageing hippies who claimed to be avatars and gurus. In most cases, the so-called 'enlightened ones' encourage you to learn their own particular system of meditation. Once I was taught how to repair my aura. Apparently it was torn. The practice consisted of listening to taped music, visualizing a threaded needle and sewing with rainbow thread two inches from my body. What nonsense! I never did return to the class after that, so from now on my aura will just have to go to the invisible menders!

In today's spiritual supermarket, you can buy into anything from acupuncture to Zen. It is easy to attain certificates in most complementary therapies as well as attend courses in mediumship and all the various types of meditation. I'm not knocking these practices or their true practitioners. It is more to do with the people who market them in western countries. Glossy magazines, colourful pamphlets and business cards are handed out at psychic fairs and seminars, and even though there are many sincere people working in the spiritual supermarket, there are still those whose only objective is to make money from those in need.

With this in mind, I decided that I couldn't afford to buy spirituality. Nor did I wish to. After attending a few more of the ridiculous meditation classes, I was fortunate to meet a proper Tibetan Buddhist, Dronma, the psychic artist. It was this very humble lady who introduced me to the practices of her beautiful religion.

What I most admired about the Tibetan ways was how understated they were. I was able to assess their simplicity through spending some time with the Tibetans at the Samye Ling Tibetan temple in the Scottish borders. The temple is an exact replica of its namesake in Tibet. It is set in a beautiful valley not far from Lockerbie, a village better known because of the terrible plane crash caused by terrorists. With its Oriental-style golden roof, the ornately decorated temple is the heart centre of this peaceful community. But it is the Tibetan Buddhists who work and practise their religion there who complement the rugged scenery with gentle harmony.

Whenever you want to know the truth about any religion, all you have to do is to watch those who practise it with sincerity. One example of how down to earth the Tibetans are was shown to me when a young lady turned up at Samye Ling claiming to be possessed by demons. On arrival, she demanded to speak with one of the lamas, who, at the time, was digging in the garden with some of the monks. The small shaven-headed man, clad in wine-coloured robes, joined her almost at once. On hearing her story, he decided not to order any kind of exorcism or ritual, but simply told her to dig the garden. Then she was sent off to clean the kitchen and so on for the rest of the day.

The following day, the lama visited the now physically exhausted woman to see if she was still possessed. Needless to say, she was too tired to think about such nonsense. As is the case with most so-called 'demonic possessions' and other such fearful imaginings, she had been living in her imagination for far too long and the best remedy for this was to get back to the real world and to become well grounded.

The lack of complication among the Tibetans really inspired me to try to keep my feet on the ground. Spirituality, the Tibetan way, is simplicity itself. Their prayers and meditations are always dedicated to those in need. But more than this, the practical kindness that is common in this true temple of light was a reminder to me that even though my childhood lacked spiritual doctrine or dogma, the people who brought me up were as spiritual as any member of any religious group. This was due to their actions, not their training. My parents were compassion personified and many of our neighbours were just as likely to help another without question of reward.

Once again, I found that the answers I was seeking in my adult life lay somewhere in my past. One of the most vivid memories I have of religion came from my childhood. I remember sneaking into the Roman Catholic church at the end of our street. This grand building seemed huge to me. It was one of my favourite places. I can still recall the gruff voice of the old priest as he would expel me. 'Right, Smith, get yourself out of here. You don't belong in God's house,' he would yell. He was quite right, too, because normally I would have been trying to steal the candles from the large box at the side altar!

On one occasion, I remember slipping into the chapel during a wedding service. It was always a great day in our street whenever there was a wedding there. All the local children would gather outside the chapel gates waiting for the cars to leave, as it was a tradition for the wedding party to throw money from the car windows as they drove off.

On this particular day, I hid at the side of the large hall. There were many statues and colourful paintings on the walls, but the statue that caught my attention was one of the Blessed Virgin. Her eyes seemed to be looking straight at me. As I met that gaze I felt a great sadness and yet there was also a peaceful feeling moving up from my feet. I could feel my eyes filling with tears as I wanted to take away the pain that seemed to come from behind her eyes. I think she reminded me of so many women I knew who had the same look of resignation and tiredness on their faces – my mother, my aunt and so many women of that same generation whose lives were anything but easy. At that moment, I could have cried for the sadness of every woman in the world.

It was a strange experience for a young boy to have and it had a great effect on me. For one thing, I stopped stealing from the chapel. Just the very thought of those eyes gazing deep into my soul was enough. I also believe that it was my first experience of empathy. From then on, I began to look at people differently.

As I think about the many people around me in my early life, I am reminded of the wisdom and true spirituality that were displayed on a daily basis. If someone had a problem, they simply went with it to an older member of the community. Usually, it would be one of the older women who had come through just about every difficulty life could throw at her. She would be the equivalent of every type of counsellor that is available today. It was her life experiences that were her training, not a textbook. The other great advantage of those times was that however little money there was, there was never a reluctance to share with those in need. There was often more spirituality in the tenements of Glasgow than in its churches. All the spiritual lessons that I needed were around me.

Whenever I need reminding of this, I think of those very wise and kind-hearted souls who fought through life and still managed to give so much of themselves. One example was Effie Ritchie, a spiritual healer in our church. She didn't have much, but what she had was yours for the taking. Effie gave the distinct impression that she was very tough, although the toughest thing about her was actually the life she endured. She had lost many members of her family, including her beloved husband

Charlie, when I first met her. Not too long after this, she was told she had cancer of the stomach.

I am never so amazed as when I meet someone with a terminal illness who seems to give strength to those around them rather than receive it. Effie was one of those people. Despite everything, she was always able to make others laugh. One of the most amusing memories I have of her is of when I went to visit her after she had just undergone major surgery to remove the cancer from her abdomen. When I arrived, she was still asleep as a result of the anaesthetic. As I stood and watched from the foot of her bed, she seemed to stir. 'Hullo there, son,' she whispered in a pathetic tone.

'Hello, Effie,' I answered, trying to smile at her. She really did look as though she had come through the wars.

At the same time, a young Asian doctor arrived at Effie's bed and had a look at the chart hanging on the top of the frame above her head. The poor woman turned her head toward the young doctor and let out a sigh.

Oh dear, I thought, *she must be suffering.*

Just then, Effie's right hand, which was attached to a drip at the side of the bed, lifted up toward the unsuspecting young man's groin area.

'Mrs Ritchie!' he shouted, directing a startled look straight at her face.

In a feeble little voice, Effie replied, 'Oh, doctor, give a dyin' wuman a brek!'

I immediately burst out laughing, but the doctor took a bit longer to get the joke. This was typical of the woman and I am sure she only behaved in this way to make me feel better, as she was never one to look for sympathy, no matter what situation she was in.

Effie lived for almost five years after this operation and it may have been her unbelievable attitude that helped her to survive for so long – or it could well have been as she described it the week before she passed away.

'Son, I was ready to go five years ago,' she said. 'Since then, I have constantly asked God why He has kept me in this world. It's only just dawned on me that I had to suffer so long to end up looking the way I do now so that my family could let me go.'

It is strange how some people have to suffer in this world. But I believe that because of it others can learn and maybe suffer less as a result.

Effie Ritchie was one of the most spiritual beings I have ever encountered in my life. This was not because she could give profound answers to questions relating to the meaning of life. Nor was she the most saintly woman. It was more to do with her compassion for others, her natural consideration and how brave she could be when faced with adversity. She became spiritual not because she tried to be, but because it was her way.

Whenever Mrs Primrose asked Effie to close our church service in prayer, some people would be so affected by the honesty of her words that they would be moved to tears. Effie always spoke to God in her broad Glaswegian dialect, as if she knew Him on a personal level: 'God, gonnee help aw ra peepil that ur suffurin, an aw the poor wee kids that don't huv much in their wee lives. God be wae au them that's no goat a bed this night, thanks God. Ah no yil dae the best ye kin. Thanks.'

And she meant every word of it. It is my prayer that God will pray as hard for Effie as she prayed for others. May He bless her.

I believe I have discovered the best place to begin looking for spirituality: within myself. Religions and philosophies can steer us towards spiritual enlightenment, yet it is up to each one of us to discover our own spiritual nature.

Spirituality can neither be bought nor sold. It can only grow in this world or remain hidden. The choice is ours. Every day life puts lessons in front of each of us. We can choose to learn our lessons or ignore them. We can choose to live in a world made more harmonious by what we do or one that is filled with ignorance that we leave unchallenged.

If you can, remember kindness.

CHAPTER FOURTEEN

When I had worked the length and breadth of the UK, I thought that I had done it all. Not so, it would seem. The next challenge for my mediumship was to be found overseas. Abroad! Me? How would I pass on messages in a foreign language? How would I be understood, even though I'd now adopted the upmarket accent of North Kelvinside, the best part of Glasgow?

This new opportunity to expand my mediumship was due to my old friend Albert Best. Albert thought so highly of my clairvoyant abilities that he recommended me to churches and societies abroad as well as up and down this country. In a short time, I had offers of work in such places as Australia, America, Germany, Switzerland, Spain and Gibraltar.

There was no way I could accept all these

offers due to work commitments at home. The only thing to do was to choose those that would fit in with my already overloaded schedule. It so happened that the only dates that would fit into my diary were those in Spain and Gibraltar. Once I had accepted the offer, I wondered just what I had done. This would be the greatest test of my psychic abilities so far – would I come through it a more accomplished medium?

When I arrived at Malaga Airport, I was greeted by Ray and June Smith, who run the Gibraltar Psychic Research Society. For the next week I lived with this very kind couple in their beautiful villa in the picturesque hills of Santa Margarita in southern Spain, overlooking Gibraltar. During that week I gave 35 private sittings as well as two public demonstrations of clairvoyance. Everyone seemed pleased with my style of mediumship. The Spanish and Gibraltarian people who received spirit communications all reported favourably on the evidence they were given. If there was a problem, it was only that most of the electrical equipment I came into contact with broke down. This was highlighted by Ray when he reported on the week's events:

Not only did the microphone fail to work each time Gordon held it, but our video equipment failed to capture any pictures at all. Furthermore, our audiotapes quit; they just ceased the moment the medium began to work.

This is why I have no reports of what occurred on my first visit!

My second trip to the Rock was even more successful than the previous one. This time my demonstration in the John Macintosh Hall was captured on audio, though even after many checks, the video equipment still failed to work on the night.

The following is the report *Psychic News* later ran on its front page, under the headline 'Glasgow Medium Gordon Smith Rocks Them in Gibraltar':

Ray and June Smith from the Gibraltar Psychic Research Society report that Scottish medium Gordon Smith made an immense impact on the Rock of Gibraltar this month.

In one contact, the medium asked whether anyone knew the name Miguel, who had been killed in Red Sands Street. A lady responded, saying that Miguel was her brother, and that the name of the road was Red Sands Road, not Street. As the medium gave the numbers 1–1, the lady understood.

'He's telling me that he will be close to you on March 15,' continued Gordon. 'That's my birthday,' replied the lady. The medium surprised the recipient by telling her that she would enjoy herself in Australia. The lady told Gordon she had planned to go in the

springtime.

'He has brought with him a young boy,' Gordon said. 'About one year old.'

'That's my son,' replied the lady.

The recipient of this wonderful message was naturally in tears, overcome with emotion as she listened to the medium.

Gordon went to another woman saying, 'I have your niece here, who tells me she was killed in an accident five years ago.'

The lady confirmed this, saying that she was her aunt. The medium continued, telling the lady she was wearing the rings that belonged to her niece.

Gordon described how the communicator was telling him that the niece was looking after Maria. The recipient replied, telling the medium that Maria was the mother of her niece.

Finally in this communication, Gordon gave the name Eva, and said that Eva was 17 years old and that her mother was starting to feel better about her.

Ray Smith states: 'I know Eva's mother because in the past she has come to many meetings both in the centre and in the theatre. The mother's name is Marie Carmen, and she has been grieving ever since she lost her daughter in a motor accident.

'The contacts quoted are only a sample of

those the medium gave. All the links made in both demonstrations, as well as in his private sittings, were of the same very high standard.

'I can assure you we have recordings and many witnesses to verify that all that has been reported here took place. I must confess I have not witnessed such good mediumship since the days when Gordon Higginson [another top UK clairvoyant] and Albert Best came to demonstrate in Gibraltar.

'In a sense, it seemed that Albert Best was helping Gordon with his mediumship. This is not surprising since they both lived in Glasgow, and Gordon has worked with Albert.

'In the opinion of the Gibraltar Psychic Research Society, Gordon Smith's mediumship was very good on his last visit here, but on this occasion he has surpassed himself. The request for his return was shared by all in the theatre when at the end of the meeting he received a wonderful ovation.'

What wasn't in that report was the fact that I had to go on local television and do battle with a priest who had announced on the radio news that the Devil had arrived in Gibraltar in the form of Gordon Smith from Scotland!

If that wasn't enough attention, June Smith asked me if, for effect, I would wear a kilt on the night of the theatre demonstration. Wearing a kilt is one thing, but then I learned that we were to travel over from the Spanish side on a 750cc motorbike, with me riding on the back. Were the Gibraltarians ready for this?

I had never worn a kilt while riding on a motorbike before, so had no idea that it would be lifted up over my head, making me resemble a rather large red tulip speeding along at 50 miles an hour. The Spanish guards at the checkpoint were wide-eyed, to say the least, when the Devil arrived wearing a red dress! Still, once we eventually got to the theatre, the people really did appreciate the Highland dress, although, being a true Scot, it disturbed me that I could have been arrested for high-speed flashing!

Working with the Spanish and later the German people helped me to gain even more trust in spirit communicators. It showed me that even language differences do not pose a problem for those on the Other Side, for messages of love and comfort were passed to relatives as clearly and accurately as they are in the United Kingdom.

All of my life I have noticed that even the most unlikely predictions have come to pass. So when I was asked to visit Japan to represent the Spiritualist Association of Great Britain (SAGB), I simply remembered the prediction given to me by that wise old medium Albert Best, who three years earlier had said, 'You will visit Japan within the next five years.'

I should explain that the SAGB is housed in a

beautiful Georgian building in the heart of London's Belgravia. I often appear there when the Association is holding a special public event, and love demonstrating in the Oliver Lodge Hall with its grand piano, glittering chandeliers, original Adam fireplaces and large windows overlooking Belgrave Square. Of course, as well as seeing friends old and new, it is also a marvellous opportunity to meet up with fellow mediums from throughout the United Kingdom. Another of the delights of serving the Association is the feeling of warmth and camaraderie between all who serve there. I really do regard it as a great privilege to call myself an SAGB medium.

But back to Japan. On 25 April 1999, I flew to Japan with Hiroshi Kinjo, a spiritual healer at the Association. As well as being my interpreter, Hiroshi would give healing and lead some of the workshops. These involved spiritual awareness and healing.

Before we began our nine days' spiritual work, Hiroshi took me on sightseeing trips to many of the most beautiful parts of Japan. We also had time to visit some of the old Buddhist, Shinto and Zen temples dotted throughout the countryside. For me, these visits were the highlight of my sightseeing. Each temple was more beautiful than the last, all of them built in the traditional Japanese style, with gold sloping roofs and exquisite carvings and paintings. Equally as fantastic were the sculpted gardens that surrounded them. I spent much of my time trying to picture the ancient peoples in their colourful costumes and robes roaming about these picturesque places, mindfully going about their duties.

These peaceful temples with their gardens and backdrop of ghostly high mountains shrouded in mist and low cloud were a complete contrast to the bustling streets of Tokyo. Here, the buildings seemed as tall as mountains and the streets were aglow with neon signs of all colours. All were crammed with millions of people going about their business like droves of ants. From the top of the fairly high building where we were staying, I looked down on some of the main streets of this vast city and was amazed at the view below me. If Tokyo was the heart of Japan, these great floods of people flowing through its streets were the blood pumping around its veins. In all my life I have never witnessed so many people in one place at one time. And they seemed to be as concentrated on their business life as the monks in the temples were on their spiritual practices.

During the course of our spiritual work, many people came along to take part in workshops, spiritual healing and demonstrations of clairvoyance. To our delight everyone appeared to enjoy themselves at each event.

For me, the most amazing aspect was being able to hear and correctly pronounce the Japanese names of spirit contacts. As I do not speak Japanese and 99 per cent of the recipients had no English, this proved to be a great help. As always, the spirit people proved that they could bridge the language gap.

Of all the many messages given in public and private sittings, there is only one that sits at the front of my mind. It happened on the second to last day of our work schedule. Everything had gone well. In fact it couldn't have gone any better, Hiroshi and I were just saying to one another. Why is it that whenever you have that thought, someone or something turns up to change it?

It was the last sitting of the day. Our sitter was a gentleman in his mid-fifties, who was very well groomed and smartly dressed. I had just begun to tune in when he started to speak in a rather hurried fashion to Hiroshi. My interpreter turned to me and said, 'He believes he has been possessed by an alien.'

I looked at Hiroshi in amazement. Apparently, the alien was lodged between the man's testicles and liver. He told us he had swelling around both parts of his body and that his stomach would also swell from time to time.

Hiroshi was asking me what we should advise when the man began to speak again. He went on for some ten minutes or so, explaining how the alien had been transferred to him from a Japanese mystic. He seemed to be very well versed in mystical terms, as if he had read many books on the subject. I told Hiroshi to advise him to see a doctor rather than a medium. Hiroshi passed this message to the man … who then told him that he *was* a doctor!

On hearing this, I almost laughed out loud. Instead, I prescribed 'nil by mind'. I believed this gentleman to be suffering from spiritual indigestion as a result of reading too many books on mysticism and spiritual enlightenment. It was my opinion that he should try to ground himself by living as ordinary a life as possible. I ended the session by offering the poor soul spiritual healing in the hope that he would feel more relaxed and maybe see his condition in a different light.

Apparently, it worked. As soon as the healing was finished, he announced that the alien had been reduced to one-sixteenth of an inch.

It is difficult to imagine that someone so intelligent could delude themselves in such a way, although I found many of the people we saw in Japan to be very superstitious. Several of them came to me in hope that I might be able to break curses put on them or their family members. In all of these cases, all I could offer was common sense.

All things considered, my trip to Japan was a fascinating experience, even though I was very tired at the end of it. No matter where I go in this world or how enticing a place can be, it is always good to get back home.

But as for resting, there was no chance! I

practically stepped off the plane and onto the platform. Luckily for me I was sharing it with the brilliant young medium from Essex, Tony Stockwell. Tony and I seemed to work very well together. At the end of our demonstration, he turned to me and said, 'Did you know that you will go back to Japan?' A look of exhaustion came over my face. Tony smiled and said, 'I'm just kidding.' Thankfully, he was.

CHAPTER FIFTEEN

Of Seances And Sons

'I was the best of kids, I was the worst of kids.' I think that someone else wrote something like this once before, but was referring to times. As for me, in my mother's eyes I could do no wrong. Nor could any of her other children, for that matter. If any of us had smashed all the windows in every house in our street, Mum would have said, 'It couldn't have been any of mine. It must have been kids that looked like them.' If she was guilty of anything, it could only be of loving and protecting her family. And, of course, she did, like a lioness protecting her cubs. God help the person who tried to interfere with her family.

By the time I reached my early teens, there was a noted difference around our once very busy home. Both my sisters, Betty and Joan, as well as my eldest brother Tommy, had by now married and moved into their own houses. This left Sammy, John, me and my parents at home. (People sometimes ask me how I can be a seventh son when I have only five brothers and sisters, however there was another sister, Agnes, who died before she was two, hence making seven children in all.)

Sammy was just about to be given a room of his own when it was announced that Barney, my mother's father, was coming to stay, as he could no longer live on his own. My grandad was quite ill. Indeed, he was now confined to bed. He was put up in our middle room, the smallest of the three bedrooms in our house, which meant that Sammy would still have to share with John and me.

The three of us used to drive my mum mental. We would play together for so long, then one of us would disagree about something or other and the fights would start. 'Would you lot keep it down in there!' Mum would bawl. 'It's him, Mammy,' one or other of us would yell back. 'Ah don't care whit wan it is,' she'd reply. 'I'll come in there and belt every wan o'ye.'

Usually at this point we would shut up as asked, for Mum was one of those women who carried out her threats to the letter. It was no wonder, I suppose, when you consider that she was always busy cooking, cleaning and washing, mostly for other people. The last thing she needed was countless distractions from three rowdy teenagers. 'Why don't you all go outside and gie me peace fur a while?' she would ask.

One Saturday night after obeying Mum's orders to go outside and play, my two brothers and I decided to get some other friends and try to hold a seance in the old wooden hut that Sammy had built in our back garden. This experimental seance was, of course, my idea, with me as the medium. Who else? Two more of our friends joined us, making a gathering of five eager young minds hoping to pull back the veil into the Great Unknown.

We all sat cross-legged on the cold dirt floor of the shoddily constructed hut. In the centre, there was a candle welded to an upturned soup can, flickering constantly from the many draughts whistling in through gaps in the uneven planks of wood that made up our walls. The setting, I decided, was perfect for my debut as the great mystical medium forecast by Sadie and Ella. Even the weather was perfect, as the night was dark, with a slight chill in the air.

'Shush,' I moaned. 'If you want me to do this, you'll all have to concentrate.' Silence filled the hut as I closed my eyes and addressed the space above my head. 'Is there anybody there?' I said in a serious voice. I swear you could have heard a pin drop. 'If you're there, give us a sign.'

This carried on for a few more moments, separated only by silence. The intensity grew. Here I was commanding everyone's attention, only there seemed to be no backup from the spirit world. It was time to improvise.

'I can hear a voice,' I said, pretending of course. 'It's Sarah.'

Then the strangest thing did happen. As I continued with my charade, I began to speak spontaneously.

'I am coming to collect Barney,' I said in an unfamiliar voice.

'Whit diz that mean?' Sammy asked.

'I don't know,' I replied.

'You better pack this in,' he said, sounding really annoyed as he raised himself to a squatting position, which was all that the hut would allow. Then he pushed past me and left.

John looked at the two others and said, 'It's all a load of crap anyway. He just made it up.'

'The spirits don't lie,' I protested.

'Naw, but you dae!' John exclaimed.

The three remaining sitters burst out laughing and left one by one. Here I was, the 11-year-old medium, left sitting in my empty seance room. Would my brothers would tell Mum what I'd done? How could I have been so stupid to have said what I did?

The following morning, our bedroom was filled with light blazing in through the large double windows. John and I awoke almost at the same time. We decided to go down to the living-room and play with our table football game, agreeing to keep the noise down, as the rest of the family was still asleep. Typically, though, within five minutes or so we had woken everyone up. 'Would you two keep the noise down in there!' my mother shouted from the far end of the house. I immediately tried to mimic her voice. 'Shut up, you! She'll hear you,' John scolded me.

The two of us were trying to muffle our laughter and still keep the game going when suddenly there was a scream. John and I were rooted to the spot. It felt as if a siren had gone off and we were waiting for the next sound to release us from our fear. Within seconds everyone was in the hall – Sammy had jumped out of bed, John and I were rushing out of the living-room, my father was just coming out of Grandad's bedroom and Mum was standing at the door of her bedroom, at the end of the long hall, tears streaming down her face.

Dad had got up to make a cup of tea for Mum and Grandad, and Mum had been listening to him trying to rouse her father when something inside her told her that he had died. 'He's dead, isn't he?' she said.

I had never seen my mother sad before. Somehow, I felt responsible. If I hadn't held that stupid seance the previous evening, none of this would have happened. The look of shock on the faces of my two brothers filled me with a kind of remorse. *Oh dear*, I thought. *What will I say if they repeat what happened last night?*

I didn't have to be psychic to understand the

seriousness of what was happening now. Dad immediately sent the three of us to my sister. Betty lived around the corner from us, no more than a minute's walk from our house. Her husband Jim stayed with us while my sister ran round to my parents to be with my mother while Dad sorted things out. As the three of us sat there, I could tell by the looks I was getting that my two brothers weren't going to say anything about my prediction, although I believe it was out of fear. I am sure they thought I was evil at that moment.

Shortly after my grandad's funeral, Dad began redecorating the middle room so that Sammy could move into it as soon as possible. John and I argued that we wanted a room of our own – just because Sammy was the eldest, why should he have it? Sammy just sneered at us from behind Dad's back. Meanwhile Dad pointed out to us it was only right the eldest should have it. How quickly life goes on. It was only a week since Grandad's funeral and there we were debating to see which one of us should get his bedroom.

As far as I was concerned, the matter was not yet closed. Although I was the youngest in the family, I had a plan that would see me replacing my elder brother in that room! My idea was to frighten my brother with the thought of my grandad's spirit still hanging around it. The first night Sammy slept there I scratched the adjoining wall of the bedrooms, trying to make just enough noise to keep him awake. Children really can be horrible to one another!

My plans were given a real boost one day when the three of us were alone in the house together. In Sammy's bedroom there was an old-fashioned wardrobe with two really heavy walnut doors. These were always kept locked, as the weight of them when not secured made them creak open. Whilst the others were in the living-room watching our new colour TV, I crept into the middle room, unlocked the wardrobe doors, switched on the radio and tiptoed quickly to the toilet.

'Get oot ay that room, you, ya we pig,' Sammy shouted.

'I'm in the bathroom,' I called back in my most innocent tone.

Just then, I could hear Sammy's heavy steps coming to check up on me. This was followed by a terrifying scream of 'Barney!' More footsteps. This time, he was joined by John. Both of them made for the front door, past the toilet where I was lying in wait. Realizing that I would be left in the house by myself, I threw open the bathroom door, screamed 'Ah … ah … ah,' and fled with my brothers to the safety of my sister's house. I suppose I got caught up in the drama that I had created.

Imagine the fright my sister got when the three of us battered at her door demanding to be let in. 'It's Barney! A ghost! He was coming to get us!' We blurted out all kinds of ridiculous things, hoping she would believe us.

'It wiz ma Granda,' Sammy said.

'A seen um, Betty,' John chipped in.

'Aye, so did ah!'

Betty turned to me, asking, 'Did you huv any thin tae dae way this?'

'Naw, Betty,' I said. 'A wiz in the toilet. Bit ah seen um as well, so a did.'

By the time we had finished, it was beginning to sound like something out of *The Amityville Horror*.

Betty accompanied us back to the house. The front door was still wide open. After she had gone round and checked that everything was alright, she reassured us that we had not seen the ghost of my grandfather, but that it was all in our imagination. She told us not to tell our mum of this event, as it would upset her, and that there were no such things as ghosts.

In fact, when my mum came home from shopping, the ghostly episode was forgotten almost at once, as the contents of her shopping bags were much more interesting. 'Did you get us anything in town?' was all we wanted to know.

But later that evening, as we were getting ready for bed, there was a strange reluctance on Sammy's part to enter his bedroom. I wonder why!

'Da, a think I'll sleep in wae them tonight,' he said.

'Whit's wrang wae you?' Dad asked.

'A don't like that room,' Sammy replied.

'Kin a huv it, Da?' I chirped.

'Well as long as somebody sleeps in it, a don't care,' said Dad.

It was done. I had it. And from then on it was mine until we moved house some five years later. The scheming little 'psychic' got his way ... eventually.

I now have two sons, Paul and Steven. Both show signs of having psychic abilities, though it has never occurred to me to point this out to either of them.

Paul, the elder, is 21 and studying history at Glasgow University. He takes great pleasure in explaining to me how all my work can be put down to chance or probability. He often says things like, 'Dad, if these people believe what you tell them, then good, but really I'm surprised you actually believe that spirit entities are speaking to you.' At 21, we think we know it all! But even the very scientific Paul changed his mind when he came to watch me demonstrate at the university in front of his peers.

Steven, who is 18, is a more artistic young man. He has a great love for art and drama, and likes to take part in all kinds of sport. Steven is a more sensitive kid. Throughout his childhood, he displayed both psychic and telepathic gifts.

I remember one occasion when driving past the Hilton Hotel in Glasgow. Steven, who was only ten at the time, suddenly said, 'I wonder what it's like in room 1308?' I asked him why that particular room. All Steven could say was that he 'saw' the number appear in front of him when he looked at the hotel.

We gave no more thought to the matter and carried on with our previous conversation. It wasn't until a week later that I realized that Steven's vision of the number 1308 was, in fact, a premonition, for I was invited to the Hilton to give a private sitting to one of the guests … who happened to be staying in room 1308. Considering all the rooms in a hotel of that size, I wonder what the chance would be of guessing that.

Kate, my ex-wife, and I did not always agree on psychic matters. But one thing we did completely agree upon was that neither of us would influence the children with our own systems of belief. Both our sons are very sensitive and clever. They each display compassion in their own ways. We felt that as long as they were cared for, and felt loved and guided in their lives, they could decide for themselves which religious paths they would follow – or not, as the case may be – when they were old enough to choose.

I am a great believer in not making a fuss if you notice psychic ability in your child. Neither should you scold them for it. Kids have enough to contend with growing up without ideas of other dimensions filling their minds. They have such fertile imaginations and can invent so many fanciful episodes that it can become difficult to know what is psychic and what is imagination anyway. If a child truly has mediumistic abilities, the gift will grow with age as with any other gift, like a talent for art or music.

As a medium, life can be strange, sometimes even lonely. I, for one, hope that my children express their gifts in this world in other ways, but most importantly, in their own individual ways.

CHAPTER SIXTEEN

Animals In The Spirit World

'Do animals go on to the spirit world?' Mediums are often asked this question. I have no doubt that they do. During my time as a medium, I have passed evidence of animal survival to many people.

Don't get me wrong – I'm not suggesting that animals come and talk to me. I mean, I'm not some kind of Dr Doolittle to animals in the spirit world. But more often than not, when a spirit communicator passes information to a friend or loved one, they mention their beloved pets that are with them on the Other Side.

One of the most difficult things I had to do in recent years was take my old Labrador, Elsa, to the vet to be put to sleep. I remember thinking, 'Of all people, I should be able to handle this situation. No problem!' How wrong I was. The moment I looked down into Elsa's big brown eyes as the vet was about to administer the fatal injection, quite frankly I could feel such a lump in my throat that I thought I would choke. When I was asked if I would like to say any last words, I had never before experienced such emotion in a single moment.

The feeling of responsibility was enormous. For the rest of that day I was so depressed, wondering if I had done the right thing. I couldn't help but think of Elsa's beautiful golden face staring up at me, with those deep, dark, sad puppy eyes of hers. What a terrible and traumatic day.

That evening, I was to take the service at Kilmarnock Spiritualist Church. The very last thing I wanted to do was to stand up in public and speak to people, but after a lot of thought I decided to go to Kilmarnock. Yet even as I sat on the platform, listening to the Chair announce my name, all I could think of was Elsa.

On most occasions when I am about to work, the feeling of the Spirit moving through me just before I speak fills me with energy and inspiration, and this was no exception. All thoughts emptied from my mind and I was soon giving messages to people in the congregation.

The last message of the night is the only one I can remember. I was directed to a lady at the back of the large church. After she accepted the contact from the spirit world, I was suddenly aware of a dog sitting beside her. I told her about this and she started to sob. As the message progressed, it became clear that not long ago she had had to have her dog put to sleep. Here I was telling this woman that her beloved pet was fine in the spirit world, that it looked so young and full of life, and I had just gone through the same agony of saying 'Adieu' to a much-loved pet.

At the close of the message, the woman was given the news from her mother on the spirit side that she had indeed done the proper thing for the animal as it had been suffering quite a bit of pain, much like Elsa. I took great comfort from this message. But strangest of all, the dog in question was a Golden Labrador, the same as Elsa. The timing of the spirit people is really quite amazing, don't you think?

It has often been said that our pets give us unconditional love. It is that vital bond of love that transcends the so-called 'vale of death'. Why should it matter if that love is forged between two people or a person and an animal? There is a lot we could learn from the animal kingdom about love. Love is instinctive. Animals do most things by instinct. Of all the pets I have been privileged to have in this life, there is not one that I can say I loved more than the others. Each had its own personality, its own consciousness. After all, it is consciousness that survives physical death, so why shouldn't the personalities and consciousness of sentient animals, like domestic pets, live on and indeed progress spiritually, as we do?

I, and so many other mediums, have given evidence to people about the continued life of their pets in the spirit world countless times. I have received hundreds of letters of thanks from grateful people saying how uplifted they felt to hear that their pets were in the spirit world and to know that on certain occasions they have visited them from the Other Side.

I have seen spirit animals so many times. I have heard them and sensed them. I even had an out-of-body experience once when I found myself surrounded by dogs in the spirit world, some of whom I recognized. All seemed very friendly toward me. I have even been privileged enough to touch spirit animals and feel their soft warm fur beneath my hand. What's more, to feel the love they radiate is truly something else.

I could cite countless cases of my encounters with animals on the spirit side and I find just as much joy and satisfaction in reuniting people with their pets as with their human partners and friends. All I can say is this: if you accept that the spirits of men and women live on after death, is it so hard to imagine that animals also continue? For I believe that once the precious life-giving spark of spirit enters into an animal – be it a much-loved cat, goldfish, budgerigar, name what you will – nothing, not even death, can vanquish it. Spirit is indestructible, no matter what its form.

Looking back at my experiences, domesticated

animals, because of their close association with humans and the love given to them, develop their individuality and personality more than other species. But I am totally certain that all animals, whether of feather, fur or fin, merely move on to a higher realm when their time arrives to quit the earthly scene. And I know, too, that come the day when we pass on, our much-loved pets will be there to greet us with a wagging tail or warm and gentle purr of sheer delight. Yes, on the Other Side, the lion truly shall lie down with the lamb.

CHAPTER SEVENTEEN

Trance, Guides And Teachings

Trance mediumship is probably the most evidential form of contact given from the spirit world. The idea of a medium going into trance, giving up a part of their mind and body so that the spirit control can link in a much stronger way, should create a much clearer form of contact from the Other Side. The information coming across must surely be more precise. Any evidence, you would think, has to be more conclusive.

But the sad fact about trance communication is that not many mediums today demonstrate proper deep or controlled trance states. Over the past 12 years, I have witnessed many mediums claiming to work in trance. Unfortunately, of those I have seen, few are actually working in this very rare state.

Also, on so many occasions spirit controls talk at great length about such diverse subjects as aliens from outer space or the origin of crop circles. Some even seem to predict the end of the world. Believe it or not, I once listened to a so-called 'spirit guide' talking about her life as a dolphin. I ask you!

I find it difficult to believe that people can delude themselves in this fashion. Surely spirit people who have a chance to communicate in such a special way would say more about things that have a bearing on the lives of those they are speaking to rather than give garbled messages about strange phenomena or ridiculous situations, such as once being a dolphin.

It is because of this type of nonsense that trance mediumship comes under such attack from the sceptics. And sadly, these 'mediums' are more willing to demonstrate their charades in public than true practitioners.

Something I have come to learn about genuine mediums is this: when their gift has reached a high standard, it is often shared only with those who really need it – and, what's more, in private. Many of the best mediums refuse to work for churches or organizations for fear of being put into the same category as those who think they are good but are merely deluding themselves and their sitters. Some of the most exceptional evidence I have seen, heard or sensed has come through true trance mediums. As well as this, the simple teachings their communicators and guides offered were uplifting, comforting and wise.

Another hallmark of the genuine trance medium is that there is never any fuss when the control first links with them – no moaning, groaning or exaggerated movements of the medium's body. In fact, the whole process is simple and natural, as it should be.

For the best part of 12 years I have been fortunate to sit in a very good trance circle. None of the mediums in our circle, except me, has demonstrated their trance abilities in public. Even I have only done so on two occasions. Yet so many people have come through the circle and been privileged to share the experiences the spirit people have given freely.

As ours was a trance circle, the object was to learn to trust the Spirit by allowing communicators to overshadow us. First, through meditation, we let go of the control of our conscious mind. Then the spirit people around us filled the space with their own consciousness, 'impressing' their thoughts and sensations into our minds. It is like an intense type of telepathy in which images and feelings are picked up at the same time. The more you can let go, the more receptive you become to the spirit being's personality and image.

The discipline in our circle was patience. The idea was that each sitter would take time to forge a strong link with their spirit guide, no matter how long it took. Whenever you received spiritual impressions, they had to be tested. We had to get to know who was working with us – and if a spirit control came to speak to the group, they would have to pass certain tests too. Only when all of this was complete could you take a step forward in your development.

For the first few years, I certainly learned patience. No matter how keen I was, my spirit helpers seemed to be in no rush to make contact. Each week, in my mind I asked all sorts of questions of them, eagerly awaiting an answer. No chance!

I wasn't so stupid that I couldn't recognize a lesson in patience when it was being taught. Sometimes it was hard, but always when I got to the stage of giving up, something nice would happen. One night, for example, on the way to church to attend the circle, I decided I'd had enough of it and thought about doing something else with my time. Looking back, I suppose it was just a case of feeling a little bit down at that particular time. However, by the time I reached church, I had completely for-gotten how I was feeling. I settled down in my chair as usual and just got on with it.

Not too long into the meditation, I became aware of someone standing directly in front of me. In my mind's eye I could see the figure of a person dressed in what looked like a habit. The bizarre thing about this vision was that I couldn't see the person's head. Just then, their hands reached out toward me and I felt compelled to raise my hands toward theirs.

No sooner had the thought occurred to me than my hands were in motion, lifting up to join those of the figure before me. When they touched, I was amazed how real the hands in front of me seemed. They felt solid, warm and quite coarse. The next thing I knew, they were pulling me to my feet. During all of this, I still couldn't see the figure's head.

At this point, I began to realize that I was standing outside myself. My physical body was being worked by someone else. It was a small Chinese-looking man. He appeared to be moving my body by a process of thoughts. Meanwhile, the person I had seen first – the one dressed in a habit – seemed to be speaking, yet the words were coming out of my own mouth.

All of this happened in what felt like an instant when, in fact, 20 minutes or so had passed. The feelings I experienced during this episode were indescribable. To say that I felt lifted, exhilarated or on a high would not begin to come close to what I truly felt, but of course it had to end and I came back with a bit of a jolt.

At the end of the circle, everyone was anxious to know what had happened to me. Apparently I had got to my feet, walked across the room and up the stairs at the side of the platform, stood on the platform and spoken for some time on spiritual matters, then walked back to my seat and sat down. Of course, the voice speaking was not recognized as my own, but that of one of the spirit people who was working with me.

I described the two people I was aware of and the immense feeling of upliftment. At this point, Mrs Primrose broke in, saying, 'You were in a deep state of trance. I saw the spirit people you mentioned. They will be working with you like that for a while.'

As I tried to take all of this in, she added, 'Oh yes, I was to tell you from them that they heard you on the way to church tonight. This is their way of saying you are ready to move forward.'

By 'moving forward', the spirit helpers meant that I was ready to experience working in a trance state, and for the next couple of years I did.

As the years went by, I got to know the guides and helpers working with me. There seem to be a number of them, but my main guide is the little Chinese man I saw that night. Because I cannot pronounce his full name, I call him Chi. It would appear that Chi lived quite some time ago. As far as I am aware, he was just a humble little man. The few times I have seen him, he has always looked the same. I've never seen him dressed in magnificent robes or anything like that. Each time he comes to work with me in trance, I feel his light, wispy beard and moustache impress upon my face. Whenever he speaks through me, what he says is always so simple yet filled with grace and wisdom.

I became so used to Chi's presence I suppose it never occurred to me that any other spirit person might want to use me in this manner, which is why later on I got quite a shock. It happened one night when I was giving a private sitting to a young man not long after the death of his father. Whenever I give a private sitting to someone, I am always in complete control of my faculties. By this, I mean I never go into trance. As far as I was concerned, trance only happened in our circle, but I was about to learn another lesson: don't ever make hard and fast rules when you work for the spirit world!

The sitting started out quite well. I made contact with the young man's father and he relayed information about how he had passed over. Then I heard him saying that his name was Jimmy. None of this was out of the norm.

Just then, I became aware of a voice deep inside me telling me to relax. I started to feel light-headed. Even though I was still speaking to my sitter, I could not hear the words coming out. What happened next was strange, even for me.

I opened my eyes to see the young man sitting in front of me. His face was soaked with tears, his eyes wide with a look of astonishment.

'Are you alright?' he asked.

'Well, yes,' I replied, wondering what had happened. I knew I must have gone into trance, but that's all.

'Would you mind telling me what went on?' I asked.

'Don't you know?' said the sitter.

The fact was that I had no idea at all! Normally when I go into trance, I have some sort of awareness, but on this occasion I had been completely out of it.

According to the sitter, I was speaking to him in my normal voice about his father when he noticed that my voice was beginning to change. A voice speaking with a French accent seemed to take over. What's more, the voice was that of a woman calling herself Dominica.

The young man went on to tell me that Dominica said she was one of my spirit helpers and that she had entranced me and made contact to prove the authenticity of her life on Earth some 500 or more years ago. She told my sitter that he had just come back from the place where she had lived all that time ago, San Sebastian, in the Basque region of Spain. This, it seemed, was true. She added that he was the last person ever to be allowed to sleep in her convent. Again, this was true. While backpacking through Europe, my sitter had wandered from his original route and ended up in San Sebastian looking for somewhere to sleep for the night. The only place open to him was an old convent at the top of a mountain. It would, he was told, close the following day.

Dominica had then gone on to describe a part of the trip the young man had told no one. Apparently he had been mugged while passing through France and as his money had been stolen, he had had to spend the night in the home of one of the French police officers. Dominica asked him to tell me all of this so I could investigate some of the details in the future. Then she gave perfect evidence of the young man's father in the spirit world.

It seems that while Dominica was speaking, all the plants in the room started to shake. But it was the young man's final words that really surprised me. 'She said to tell you that she was the one who took your hands and lifted you from your seat, whatever that means.' There was no way that my sitter could have known that this incident had indeed occurred.

Dominica gave me so many things to look for about her life. It has taken me seven years to find out that she really did live back in the fifteenth century. All she said about her life was correct. She was French, but went to live in a convent in San Sebastian, where she later died as a result of her newfound beliefs. There is so much I could write about this soul, but the only person who needs to be convinced of her existence is me – and, of course, I am.

Once a spirit person gives me some kind of evidence about their earthly identity and it is verified I no longer question it or, indeed, their existence. And both Chi and Dominica have passed that test.

It is very important for any medium to check information given by their spirit helpers. Even those who teach us from the Other Side encourage us to 'test the spirits'. After all, mediums put themselves up for ridicule in the public eye. Therefore, total trust must exist between medium and guide.

As mentioned earlier, the teachings we receive from spirit mentors are so simple and filled with so much common sense. The benefits of these lessons normally come to us when we need them most. I try not to ask too much of my helpers, for I have come to understand that when they have something to teach me, I will be told. What's for you will never go past you! That is why I don't generally put myself up for public demonstrations of trance. People quite often ask so many selfish questions, thinking that those in the higher realms have the answers to all their problems. Life on Earth is just not meant to be that simple, I'm afraid. We are here to learn, and often by our mistakes, too!

Another important point is that spirit communicators do not instantly become possessed of all knowledge. Indeed, it is debatable just how far ahead they can see. Then there is the complex question of free will. We on Earth are not puppets on a string and have our own choices to make.

Sadly, if a gift like trance mediumship is on offer too frequently, some will abuse it. Like all things that are precious, some people by their very nature will want to own it.

My advice to those who seek answers through the gift of trance is this: if you feel that the trance is true and the speaker is of a higher mind, please treat them with the respect they deserve. Never be afraid to test them, but always be courteous. Listen carefully to what you are told, remembering that the voice of the Spirit would never deliberately misguide or mislead you. And be careful about what you ask – you might just get an answer!

Last – but certainly not least – always exercise your own judgement, intelligence and reason. Never embark on a course of action simply because someone in the spirit world advises you to. Those on the Other Side are still very human and can make mistakes, too. No one is infallible on either side of the so-called 'veil'.

As a medium, I never use my contact with the spirit world to help me in my life, though the trust I have built with my guides and helpers will, I hope, enable me to help many others.

During a trance demonstration Dominica gave in England, one lady asked, 'What is the greatest problem that people have in this life?'

The reply was this: 'Fear. Fear is the one major problem that humankind shares. All of our problems are born out of fear. You become afraid when you lack things, but even more afraid when you have things, fearing that you will lose what you now have. That which you fear most is death and dying. All of your life you are plagued by the thought of death, either your own or those whom you love.

'Try to accept the impermanence of the physical world in which you live. Remember that all life is in

CHAPTER EIGHTEEN

An Attorney's Account

In 1996, a friend of mine, Anthony Davidson, a solicitor in Glasgow, called and asked if I would see a friend of his from America who was going to be in Glasgow for a few days. 'Of course,' I said. All Anthony told me was his name, Richard Rosin.

We met at Anthony's house on the afternoon of 12 August and it was the beginning of a friendship that continues to this day. I will allow Richard to tell the story in his exact words:

On August 29, 1994, the most gentle, kindly-disposed young man I have ever known was brutally murdered by five cowardly predators across the street from where he peacefully resided. He was 27 years old. He was a brilliant scholar. He had wanted to devote his life to teaching young people.

In the normal course of events, he would

have married my daughter and become my son-in-law. Some 16 months later, my beloved daughter, who was his mirror image in terms of gentility and kindness, died of a broken heart, by her own hand.

She was 21 years old. She had always been a delightful and loving child. Throughout her too short life, she brought constant joy and happiness to others, believing that if you did good in the world, it would come back to you. It always had ... until that August day.

I have a Scottish solicitor friend, Anthony, who has a great interest and belief in Spiritualism. He suggested that the next time I was in London, I travel to Glasgow and meet with Gordon Smith. Although skeptical, I trusted Anthony's judgment and agreed to come to Glasgow.

On a sunny afternoon on August 12, 1996, Anthony picked me up at my hotel and took me to his house. Shortly thereafter, there was a knock at the door and a very pleasant-looking, smiling young man entered the room. His demeanor and effect were such that you immediately felt relaxed and comfortable in his presence. His name was Gordon Smith.

We sat by a large window. As the light came streaming in, filling the room, Gordon asked if he could put his hand on mine. Such was the beginning of a journey that is difficult to *explain. Its true belief lies in experiencing it for yourself.*

Gordon began a conversation that he was part of, and described what he was hearing, referring to a young woman who had recently passed into the spirit world. He mentioned a connection to Canada, a continuous and repetitive reference to law, and a year that had passed with so many changes, an incredulity that so much could happen, and a blackness attached to the year.

As Gordon continued, it was obvious that he was experiencing something highly emotional. He was perspiring in a room that was cool, and talked of dizziness, his head hurting and 'loads and loads of tears'.

Gordon continued that 'nobody expected this', talked of a ricochet, a lady dressed in a long white outfit, and a disbelief that 'she is not here'. He referred to an 'M' appearing above my head. This was the first initial of the first name of my dear daughter's beloved friend. Gordon said he heard the song 'Wish me luck as you wave me goodbye', as if he were witnessing my daughter as she began her own journey in departing this Earth to find and join her true love.

I had placed a picture on the table in front of us, but said nothing. Gordon indicated that this was the lady he saw in the spirit world, now safe, having been trapped for a time on the Earth plane. 'I am feeling a bright light,' said Gordon. 'Leaving this world there is a sense of freedom, but an anchor of pain has been left.'

Gordon could not have realized how prophetically true his revelations were. The picture was of my daughter, Beck … and the pain of a parent burying a child is unlike any other. It truly is an unnatural sequence that plummets you to the lowest level of sadness imaginable.

How could any of what Gordon related be explained? Gordon knew nothing of my daughter's untimely death, that the family of Moez, her partner in life to be, lived in Canada, of the 18-month prosecution in the American courts of the five who so brutally took the life of gentle Moez. How could Gordon have described so accurately the effect of the year of changes that were in actuality beyond the comprehension of those to whom they occurred?

I am an American lawyer, trained and schooled in an Ivy League university in finance and then law, two disciplines that demand a rigorous order and level of proof. What I had heard and witnessed defied what I could explain. And yet I knew what I had heard and seen; of this there was no doubt.

The comfort I felt from the experience was unmistakable.

I returned to Glasgow the following June and met with Gordon, only to continue this most unique and rewarding relationship. Again, we met at Anthony's house. Gordon began to talk of a powerful source of energy he was feeling. He was being taken back three months to March, which he felt was significant. This was the month of my daughter's birthday, a fact that Gordon had no way of knowing.

Gordon began to talk in almost soliloquy format and spoke of a seminar that I was to attend in the autumn. I knew of no such seminar and yet upon my return to the United States, after the passage of a few months, I was invited to participate in a seminar. There was another reference to Canada, this time in the context of: 'Have you heard from Canada recently?' My family was very close to Moez' family in Canada and we spoke to each other often.

Gordon continued by referring to a life completed, a choice to join a loved one in the spirit world and the ability to continue to help people in a world other than ours. Once again, this was an amazingly accurate recitation of a factual pattern that Gordon could not have known. And once again came comfort in hearing it.

For the second time in two summers, I had participated in something that I could not explain. Logically, there was no way Gordon could have been in possession of the information that he related to me. It was clearly coming from some place and its consistent accuracy suggested that it was beyond coincidence. Had someone related experiences to me such as I had had with Gordon, I would have been skeptical. There was no room for skepticism. I was beginning to understand. I returned to Glasgow the next summer.

It was late in the day on July 29, 1998, when I entered Gordon's residence. We sat in a room where he often meditated. There was peaceful music in the background. Gordon's dog, Charlie, quite excited by my entrance, became very calm. Gordon put his hand on mine, sat quietly, withdrew his hand, and began to speak.

Gordon described a young man standing behind my daughter in the spirit world. He said that he felt a wonderful source of energy and that his name began with the letter 'M'.

Gordon then changed the subject and told me that I would be going to Florida. Once again, Gordon was correct. It was not possible that he could have known this. In late August,

I was to speak at a national convention relating to the victims of crime. Although arrangements had been made, I had not discussed this with anyone after leaving the United States for Glasgow. Then there was another change of subject and Gordon told me that Beck was singing 'Happy Birthday' to someone whose birthday was approaching. Beck's brother, Dan, was to be 29 the next month.

What Gordon said next was more astounding than anything he had said since we met: 'Thank you for wearing my ring – it keeps me close to you. Thank you for repairing the ring.' I wear a ring that belonged to my daughter. Gordon was not aware of this. What Gordon was also not aware of was that just before I left for Glasgow, one of the stones fell out of the ring and was lost. This bothered me very much. As I did not want to travel without the ring, which was very important to me, I went to a lapidary in Philadelphia, where I live, and had the missing stone matched and replaced.

I sat in utter disbelief. There was no way to explain what I had just been told. Gordon was unaware of the significance of what he had said. He was merely delivering a message. But it was one that abundantly demonstrated to me, beyond all doubt, that there were forces and energy levels that must be accepted and that cannot be proven in any other way than by experience.

My relationship and friendship with Gordon continued, and on June 16, 1999, I found myself back in Glasgow. My next stop was to be Antibes, in the south of France, for a European Law Society meeting. I had not as yet discussed my travel plans with Gordon. All he knew was that I would be in Glasgow for two days.

Gordon picked me up at my hotel late in the afternoon and we returned to his flat. He started our time together in the same room as the year before, and began once again by holding my hand. This time he also touched Beck's ring. Gordon said that he could sense her presence, and it was very strong.

'Tell my dad I will be with him – Nice or Monte Carlo – that lovely coast.' This did not make perfect sense to me at the time as my destination was Antibes, not Nice or Monte Carlo. I had planned to spend four days in Antibes. What I did not know when I was in Glasgow was that I would change my plans in Antibes, leave after two days and travel with friends to a lovely small town on the coast called Beaulieu, midway between Nice and Monte Carlo. I had been told something would happen that I had no idea would happen and then it did happen. This is yet another level that must be accepted simply because it has occurred.

Gordon then made reference to the young gentleman in the spirit world, saying that he could still feel the pain and mentioned a connection to his parents. Moez' parents had recently moved to London and I was planning to visit them on my return from France. I had not mentioned this to Gordon either. Gordon, however, knew and communicated this to me.

When I originally called Gordon to tell him when I would be in Glasgow, he told me that he was supposed to be demonstrating at a Spiritualist church on one of the evenings and invited me to attend. I was delighted at this opportunity. After we finished our time together at his flat, we left for his scheduled appearance at the Eternal Christian Spiritualist Church in Glasgow.

Although we arrived a bit early, there were people outside waiting for Gordon. There was excitement in the air. We entered the church to find every seat taken. The same excitement that I perceived outside permeated inside. Gordon was wearing a shirt in a lovely shade of blue, and the calmness and peacefulness he radiated was reinforced by its soothing tone.

The service began with song and prayer. As Gordon began to speak, all eyes were upon him. A quiet enveloped the room. People were standing at the back and along the side.

The excitement had metamorphosed itself. Something very special was happening.

With each passing moment, Gordon delivered a message that had meaning to someone in the church. The looks of hope and anticipation turned to smiles and con-firmation. Comfort, peace, and reassurance filled the room. Gordon continued and the feelings grew. People would nod positively in response, say, 'Yes, that is right,' and accept and embrace what they heard with acquiescence. So powerful was it to observe, to be part of.

Here was a very special young man, with an extraordinarily special gift that he was sharing with all who had gathered to see him. This continued for over an hour. It was obvious that Gordon was tiring, and who would not be? He had spent a full day at his shop, then time with me and now, at the church, it was close to nine o'clock at night. The energy that was drained from Gordon as he delivered one meaningful message after another was con-siderable, and yet he unselfishly continued.

At the end of this special evening, those who had assembled were able to return to their worlds with a feeling of comfort and happiness that they did not have when they arrived. Whether a recipient or an observer, the result was much the same. Gordon provided hope, comfort, and the possibility of believing that death is not as final as it seems, that we are not as alone as we envision after the loss of a loved one, and that the spirit that is part of all of us continues after death. There is great and powerful consolation in each and every one of these concepts.

As I think about my friendship with Gordon and the meaningful effect he has on people, several thoughts occur to me. It is clear that if your mind is closed, by definition this closure precludes the acceptance and understanding of new information. By remaining open-minded to new information, we make it possible to accumulate and then learn from new experiences that we have.

It seems impossible to be able to prove by modern scientific standards what Gordon is able to convey. Yet, several centuries ago, I believe that interactions of this type were more common. And in their commonality there was greater acceptance. Science was not as capable of demanding as high a level of proof as exists today, and as a consequence it was easier for people to trust their experiences and believe in them.

I have come to believe, by my own personal experiences, that there is much we can feel and experience that cannot be explained. Much of what we feel, if allowed, can provide tremendous comfort in a situation that is too *often devoid of comfort and filled with pain, loneliness, and sadness. There is no doubt that I will never be able to explain with certitude how it is possible for Gordon to share with me what he has. And yet there is also no doubt that I know exactly what Gordon has shared with me and that it has, in fact, occurred not only in its own terms, but with repetitive clarity and accuracy. There is also no doubt as to the meaningful level of comfort and peacefulness that it has produced. Each is a very real, positive and lasting feeling that should be encouraged rather than discouraged.*

It is my belief that if we remain open to the possibility of new experiences, then they will occur and we will all be the better for them. If we remain closed to their possibility, we will guarantee their non-occurrence and fulfill a negative and empty prophecy. The choice is an individual one – I can only suggest and recommend what I myself have so clearly come to believe.

Well, I guess that's enough of being serious for now! Working constantly in such an intense area of life, you really have to learn not to get too bogged down with the emotions of others, otherwise you get washed away in the same emotional sea. After all, I am here as a kind of emotional lifeguard!

Having witnessed people's emotional pain as

much as I have, I often put the question of human suffering to the spirit world. The answer is almost the same time and again: 'It is through your suffering that you grow.'

Each one of us, it would seem, has a certain number of lessons to learn in this material life. Each individual has different lessons, although sometimes similar in nature. These lessons have nothing to do with retribution or repayment for good or bad deeds done. In fact, they have more to do with the next life than this one. They are to do with growth.

The choice is ours. Whether or not we choose to take a step towards spiritual growth depends upon how we react at critical points of our life. When you think that each major event in any of our lives is connected to one emotion or other, it would seem that the emotional part of our life is what that keeps us most earthbound, the needy part of us, the piece that wants to hold an identity for eternity. To understand your spiritual nature, you must first learn to free yourself of your emotional one. The spiritual part of you cannot be destroyed because it is connected to the God force. When we lose the physical body, it is said that the consciousness goes on. It is a series of shedding skins, if you like. We become lighter with every spiritual step we take. Physical death is only one of them.

Here I go, getting all holy and high-minded! Please just take my word for it that there is more to life than what we have now. For what it is worth, believe in yourself and try to accept the lessons of life, whatever they be.

But remember, too, that life is not merely an obstacle course set for our development. It is a gift, one to be savoured, enjoyed and lived to the very full. For as it says in the *Desiderata*, we are indeed children of the Universe, and children need light and laughter as well as training. I can do no better than end this chapter with the final words of that great manual for living: 'Strive to be happy.'

CHAPTER NINETEEN

Mediumship has taken me through many different areas of life and because of it I have met so many varied and fascinating people, none more so than those who work in the media.

Since my early days as a medium, I have often found that those in the press and on TV nearly always insist on trying to show mediumship in action. In other words, they want me to demonstrate my gifts instantly, no matter how disruptive the surroundings or hostile the atmosphere. Of course, I don't mind demonstrating for sceptics, but those who are anti-mediumship automatically create a mental – and often somewhat hostile – 'prove-it-to-me-now' barrier which is sometimes hard to penetrate. From my point of view, it's a bit like trying to climb Mount Everest in carpet slippers. Really, all I ask is that someone puts aside any preconceived notions and sits in a state of open-minded kindness and quiet expectation in the hope that I can successfully link with their loved ones Beyond. It's odd, you know. No one expects a vicar or bishop, for example, to prove that God exists, but time after time, I am put on the hot spot and asked to demonstrate the spirit world's reality in three minutes flat!

Also, presenters and journalists all tend to ask the same kind of somewhat obvious, standard questions, such as 'When did you first discover you were a medium?' or 'Can you see the spirits all the time?' I suppose this is understandable, but it would be nice to be asked some original questions once in a while.

Happily, though, the media's approach toward mediumship has changed over recent years from cynicism to a more open-minded and serious attitude.

Back in 1990 I had my first experience of television when I was asked to give an interview to a Scottish programme called *Icon*. At first, I felt very nervous about being seen by many viewers talking about my beliefs and understanding of Spiritualism. I wasn't even a fully-fledged medium at this point and here I was being asked to speak on a TV programme. I asked my teacher, Mrs Primrose, if she considered appearing on TV was a good idea. She didn't answer, just gave me a look that years later I came to realize meant a very firm 'No!'

The programme-makers were keen to film the interview in the busy salon where I worked. I suppose they wanted to show an ordinary person who by day lived a normal life cutting hair and chatting to people but by night became involved in Spiritualism.

The researchers and production team put me at ease almost at once and one of the assistant producers carried out a mock interview with me, so truth to tell, when the time came to do the interview I felt very relaxed and at ease. The young lady presenting the programme introduced herself to me and we chatted for a short while. Her name was Shareen Nanjiani and sometimes she read the news on the *Scotland Today* programme. She was very pleasant and I felt reassured ... until we began the interview!

My memory of that programme is a blur, but when I watch the video recording of it, I cringe with embarrassment. Shareen looks very much at ease, a professional putting questions – to someone who appears very wooden and looks like a man being interrogated! None of the questions put to me during the mock session came up in the filmed version. Even worse was that the direction of the interview seemed to have changed from spiritual healing and mediumship to the occult and Satanism. Of course, Spiritualism has nothing whatsoever to do with such subjects, but it is often lumped together with the more lurid, headline-grabbing aspects of the occult, even though it a recognized religion with churches throughout the United Kingdom and many other parts of the world. We also have our own ministers who, like Orthodox clerics, undergo a long period of training.

I felt absolutely shattered at the end of the interview and just wished it had never happened. Yet I was sure that the spirit world would have backed me on this. I was so positive about my feelings before it had begun. How could I have misread the situation so badly? My thoughts were all over the place. One thing was firm in my mind – I would never go on television again!

One of my greatest fears at the time was facing Mrs Primrose. I remembered the way she had looked at me when I had first told her about the programme.

'Well, how did it go, son?' she asked me.

'It was fine,' I said a little hesitantly, and probably not very convincingly.

Mrs Primrose took me by the arm and walked me into the church office. 'Now,' she said, 'tell me how you *really* feel – and be honest.'

I began to tell her how awful the whole thing had been and that I felt I had been tricked by the change of approach and line of questioning.

Mrs Primrose just looked at me again, only this time she smiled and began to explain that she knew that it would be a disaster, but that as a developing medium I had to learn to deal with such situations.

'I had to allow you to go through this lesson,' she explained. 'It is just as well it happened so early in your development.'

The only thing I could say was, 'I'll never do anything like that again!'

'Is that so?' Mrs Primrose replied somewhat quizzically, and then added, 'I think that you will, only next time you will have learned a very valuable lesson indeed, one that will stand you in good stead for the future.'

I wondered what she could mean. Would I really go back on television at some time? I was sure that I wouldn't. In fact, it would have been the last thing I would have thought about doing. It had been a terrible experience for me.

Just as I turned to leave the little office, my old teacher looked at me very sincerely. 'Gordon,' she said, with a slight smile, 'just remember this: not all the things that Spirit teaches us are pleasant. In fact, most are not, but they were right there with you all the way and will be when you do it again. Just learn to trust them. Oh – and one more thing. You never let *them* down, just yourself.'

When I left Mrs Primrose's church that night I was sure I wouldn't be doing TV again, but as ever, my teacher was correct, for it wasn't too much longer before the world of television came knocking on my door again.

One day in September 1999, one of the staff in our salon was ill and couldn't come to work. It was to be my day off, but at the last minute I received a call at home asking if I could come in. As I had no other plans for the day, I agreed.

An hour or so after I had arrived at work, a young man stopped to peer into the salon's window. It looked as though he was unsure whether or not to come inside. He seemed a little bit lost when finally he pushed open the door and asked if he could have his hair cut. He sat down in the chair next to mine and my colleague asked how he would like his hair styled.

So close are the chairs in the salon that conversations can be heard in all quarters. The young man began to chat about his work. He told the other barber that he worked for the BBC and was researching a programme where they hoped to feature the medium Gordon Smith. My ears pricked up at that moment, but I said nothing. Instead, I winked to my colleague, who understood at once that I wanted to hear more before volunteering any information.

The chap from the BBC carried on talking about his forthcoming programme and how he hoped that the medium would take part in the filming of some of the most haunted places in Edinburgh. Then he complained how hard it had been trying to find this Gordon Smith, but that he had been told he might be demonstrating his mediumship at

Glasgow University in the near future.

At this point, I couldn't resist the chance to have some fun. 'Oh, that happened two days ago, sir,' I said.

The customer turned to me.

'I heard that he wasn't very good,' I added. 'In fact, I believe he makes it all up.'

This brought an immediate response from the BBC man. 'I've heard differently,' he volunteered. 'Gordon Smith seems to have gained some respect amongst the Spiritualist community. You see, it was the people at the Spiritualist church who recommended him for our programme.'

My colleague began to smile, as did I. Eventually, I confessed to being the elusive medium. At first, the man didn't believe me, thinking that the whole thing was a wind up, but after the other barbers and some regular customers backed up my claims, he eventually accepted it.

What was more difficult for him to take in was that he had had no real intention of coming into this particular salon. He had just decided to go into the first barber's shop on his route. After he had recovered from the shock of this 'coincidence', we talked about the programme that he was putting together and what he wanted me to do.

The plan was to film some of the allegedly most haunted places in the city of Edinburgh. Using both psychical researchers and the talents of a respected medium, it was hoped to catch a glimpse of a ghost on camera or maybe gain some insight into the nature of the so-called 'hauntings'.

After much thought on my part, including a short mental consultation with my spirit friends, I agreed to take part in the programme. The filming was scheduled for that November. I found myself with a psychical researcher called Daphne and a sceptic called John being chauffeured to Scotland's capital to dredge up the past and maybe shed some light on its once plagued streets.

On our arrival at the entrance to one of the old dungeons that run beneath the city we were greeted by the film crew, the production team and Fred McCauley, the programme's presenter. Mr McCauley presents various television and radio shows in Scotland. He was being briefed on the history of the old streets by one of the city's tour guides, a young chap dressed in a top hat and long black cape.

Once all the cameras and lights were in place and Fred had gone over his script, filming began. At first, I just stood around and watched. I couldn't really say that I was sensing anything other than a damp smell and the sound of water running down the old stone walls. Daphne, however, appeared to be doing much better with a meter that registered moisture. Meanwhile, sceptic John was giving an interview to Fred about how it was all just a load of rubbish. The only person in the old dungeon to display any enthusiasm was the tour guide.

Carrying a tall church candle and swishing his long black cape for effect, he described in great detail how visitors on his tours were often scared half to death by the screams and touches of the many troubled ghosts said to haunt these tunnels.

Several hours came and went and still there was no sight of a ghost, or even a sniff of one! Eventually, we arrived at Mary King's Close, which is said to be the most haunted of all the streets. We were all tired by now and everyone's cynicism was more than apparent. It must have been at the very moment that my mind was drowning in boredom that I began to tune in to the spirit world. I remember vaguely hearing all of the ghostbusters muttering about how the energies in the close were very different from all the other dungeons and tunnels when into my mind came the voice of an elderly man. He was repeating a single word over and over again. This became so loud inside my head until eventually I said it aloud whilst staring straight at Fred.

His mouth fell open as I began to repeat word for word all that was now coming through my mind. Everyone in the dank old room fell silent, listening to this great diatribe that I was spouting in Fred McCauley's direction. All I can tell you is that it was Fred's old Grandad coming to give him a message of comfort from the spirit world.

After what seemed like an hour and yet couldn't have been more than five minutes, Fred finally said something: 'I want that tape!' He definitely didn't want the BBC to use this footage in the programme and appeared quite shaken by the whole business. I spent some time chatting to him on his own away from everyone else so that I could explain just what had occurred. Once it had all sunk in, Fred explained what it meant to him. Like most people who have never had a personal message from the spirit world before, he had so many questions. The producer told me that he would try to persuade Fred to allow him to use the footage in the programme, as he had captured a great piece of film for television. On the other hand, I felt that Fred was well within his rights to keep what was a personal message about his family well away from the prying eyes of the public.

When the series was shown, the part that featured the 'ghost hunt in Edinburgh's most haunted places' turned out to be more comical than frightening, or even informative. I suppose with people taking part with names like Fred and Daphne, it appeared more like an episode of *Scooby Doo*. Fred's message wasn't included, but after the programme had gone out all the Scottish newspapers featured stories about how he had been stunned by a message I had passed on from 'beyond the grave'. Fred himself gave some interviews saying much the same thing.

I was still undecided as to whether medium-ship belonged on television, but after all the media interest that surrounded the Fred

McCauley programme, I was invited to take part in numerous chat shows and documentaries. Some, I decided, were not for me and yet there were others that I felt would not be damaging to my mediumship. As with everything I do as a medium, I tuned in and asked the spirit world first. If the feelings that came back felt in any way negative, then I declined.

One programme that I felt would be positive was the BBC's respected *Heaven and Earth* show dealing with current affairs and religious matters that goes out on a Sunday morning. It was around the autumn of 2000 and people were still talking about the new millennium and the Age of Aquarius when filming began on a section of the show that would feature me talking and answering questions on mediumship and psychic matters. 'What harm can there be in that?' I asked myself.

The director insisted on filming me cutting the presenter's hair whilst answering his questions and describing my journey as a medium. After this interview, I was to be filmed giving a more in-depth description of Spiritualism in one of the Spiritualist churches in Glasgow. Again, what harm could there be in this? Nothing, apparently, except that a voice in my head kept telling me that the film crew was up to something.

'You aren't going to film anything in a cemetery, are you?' I asked.

'Absolutely, not!' was the reply.

'Are you certain that you don't have a plan for

me to give a private sitting to someone?'

'No, Gordon, just an interview in the church,' the director explained.

After we arrived and set things up in the church, the interview began. Presenter John Mahoney asked the usual kind of questions I had come to expect, such as 'Is Spiritualism a religion?' and 'Do many people attend the services?'

As I started to answer, I became aware of a spirit person standing at my side. I said nothing, but just kept answering the questions. Then John asked if I could connect to the Other Side for him. At this point, the director was insisting that I try to do so. It felt as though I was being goaded into performing for them.

I tried to hold back the spirit person I could feel getting stronger when all of a sudden I burst out with the name and address of my spirit communicator – much to the astonishment of one of the lighting men, who almost let go of the large light he was holding above a camera. There was no stopping now! The director was calling out for a response from the man in question, but he just stood there looking at me in much the same way that Fred had done almost a year before.

As the message poured out and the information became more and more specific, the spirit contact became very emotional, so much so that I called a halt to the whole proceedings so that I might continue in private with the unsuspecting member of the film crew.

The feature went out as part of *Heaven and Earth* some weeks later ... without the section including the message for the lighting man. Once again, I had given a very accurate and in-depth message from a loved one in the spirit world and yet it wasn't allowed to be shown on television. In a sense I was disappointed, yet again I had to agree that the message was personal and not really for the eyes and ears of the viewing public. I do regard mediumship as sacred and spirit messages as confidential unless they are given at a public demonstration of clairvoyance. Even then, I always take care not to cause someone embarrassment or breach a confidentiality. I believe that, like doctors and priests, what is said to a medium should not be broadcast – in this case literally – to others.

Part of the programme did feature a clip of the BBC presenter standing in a graveyard asking, 'Will Gordon have a message for me?' So much for that promise! Other than that, the programme was fine. It showed the interview in the salon and then studio guests discussing the subject of mediumship. I was very pleased that the episode with the lighting man was mentioned, even if they couldn't show it. What's more, the presenter commented, 'When I watched Gordon give that message, I was left with two options: that he is a very good fake or that he is a truly gifted medium. I prefer to go with the second option.' Somehow, I think that from the spirit world

Mrs Primrose would – or rather will – have approved of the *Heaven and Earth* venture!

Even so, looking back over these events it appeared to me that the world of television wasn't really ready for mediumship. On the occasions when I was able to give accurate evidence to a recipient, the footage still could not be shown. It's the same old problem that mediums have faced for many years: the moment TV producers surround mediums with people and ask them to tune in to just one person, you simply cannot guarantee it will be successful. After all, mediums cannot call up particular spirit beings, and what's more, should not do so. Spirit return is entirely voluntary and each and every attempt at spirit contact should be regarded as an experiment in two-world communication, as we are dealing with very subtle forces. It's just like tuning in a radio –unless the wavelength is exactly right you get interference, or even the wrong station altogether!

For all these reasons I decided not to be filmed doing my work on television again unless the producers could assure me that my mediumship would be shown in a surrounding that was natural to me and not something solely set up for the sake of a programme. Television may well turn out to be a part of the future for mediumship, but if that is so, I am certain the spirit world will have a big part in this. We will wait and see.

CHAPTER TWENTY

Of all of the places I have served in as a medium, there is none more rewarding than the beautiful spiritual centre in the north of Italy called Cassia del Albero. It was established some years ago with the aim of using mediumship and spiritual healing to help people who have 'lost' loved ones. Throughout the year, there are courses on how to develop and understand both healing and mediumship as well as demonstrations of clair-voyance and private sittings.

The English medium Sue Rowlands, who is very well respected in the United Kingdom and in other countries around the world, introduced me to Casa del Albero. Sue's hard work over many years has brought much comfort and healing to grieving people in all walks of life and it is because of her mediumship that several centres such as this one have been founded. I have worked with her many times and admire her no-nonsense approach, while knowing full well that she is a very compassionate person and how much this work means to her.

The first time I worked with Sue in Italy was in the year 2000. Having heard so much about the centre, I couldn't wait to see it for myself. It was founded by Carla, a lady who had suffered so badly after the death of her young son that she had taken herself along to a demonstration of mediumship that Sue had given in Italy. Sue was able to bring a great change to Carla's life by making contact with her son in the spirit world and through her beautiful centre Carla now offers grieving parents the chance to be helped in the same way. The doors of this centre are also open to sick children from all over the world – and all of this arose from just one spirit message from a son to his desperate mother.

After arriving by plane at Bologna, we were taken by car 30 or so kilometres north to a little town called Fossili, where the Casa del Albero lies in the middle of flat countryside. It is all so very different from the rugged hills and mountains that I love so much in my native Scotland. The building is a refurbished farm-type property that looks like many others we saw on our journey from the airport.

Once we were settled into our rooms, Sue introduced me to some of the people she has come to know well in her time there, and especially those who would become our right arms. By this I mean our translators, Christina, Manuela and Monica. These three very pleasant and friendly girls all had an interest in mediumship, were extremely professional and realized the importance of translation when interpreting for a medium. When you think about it, a simple word can make a massive difference to what you are trying to convey in just one sentence, let alone in what might be a fairly lengthy spirit message. I suppose you could say that translation is a form of mediumship in itself, as it involves being given information from one source and trying not to lose the essence of it while conveying it to another. Everything that I say is kept on tape for sitters, so I always try to be as deliberate as possible when working through a translator.

During our seminar, Sue and I gave talks, workshops and demonstrations of clairvoyance as well as many private sittings for those Carla felt required help. Working for people who respect both you and what you do really does make such a huge difference. Probably because of its staunch Roman Catholic culture, Italy has few mediums of its own. When you are demonstrating somewhere like that, so many people turn out to see what it's all about, along with those who need reassurance about life after death and the hope of contacting a loved one.

Of all of the work that we did in the Casa del Albero, the most fulfilling was with private sittings.

The greatest reward for any true medium is to see someone who has real need – a person who is at the end of the road, stricken with grief – and to be able to turn that around. To experience that change in a soul because of the work you have done is worth so much more than any financial gain.

Most of the people who have private sittings at this lovely centre come because they have that genuine need for mediumship and not simply to obtain psychic predictions. In any event, a medium's main role is to prove survival after death, not to forecast what the future may bring or give advice on a problem, though spirit guidance is sometimes given.

I was particularly struck by one particular sitting and can't imagine that I will ever forget it. Monica, my translator, and I walked into the small chapel at the back of the main building where I was to give my private sittings that day. Sitting waiting for us were two people, who I would guess were in their middle forties. It was a husband and wife. In Italy, a couple will very often arrive together to see a medium. But on this occasion, I didn't have to be a medium to know that they had lost a child and were seeking reassurance that somehow, somewhere, he still survived. It was very apparent, though, that the husband did not wish to be there at all. His wife kept nagging him to sit at peace and just listen. I don't speak Italian, but that sort of thing is the same in any language.

I began to tune in. 'There is a young man

here,' I said, 'who died around the age of 18...'
Monica translated. Immediately, the lady began to
cry, but her husband folded his arms, put his
chin down on his chest and looked even more
uninterested than before. The woman spoke to
him in a very agitated way. He nodded his head for
a moment and then went back to his former position.

As the sitting continued, the wife became
more and more involved. She moved to the front of
her chair and was almost leaning on top of me, just
inches away. Whenever I said something that
directly related to her son in the spirit world, she
clasped her hands together in front of her face and
looked heavenwards. I described the young man's
looks, how he was very sporting and how he died
after having an accident on his motorbike, yet
his father was still unmoved. Monica had often
commented to me that Italian men tend not to be
so demonstrative in these situations.

Looking at both parents, I could see a woman
whose face was wet with tears. Her body language
was begging to be told more about their dear son,
whom it was plain to see they loved and missed so
very much. On the surface, her husband was trying
to keep himself together, attempting to give
nothing away.

I paused for a moment and said to the young
spirit communicator, *Please, will you tell me
something that will make your father feel good?*
His reply was immediate and I began to address the

father directly, even although he avoided my gaze. 'His name,' I said, 'is Roberto.' Both parents screamed out the name simultaneously. At last, now I had the attention of them both.

I carried on by telling Roberto's father that his son wanted me to say thanks for what he had done at the football stadium in his memory. The messages were coming through so thick and fast by now that Monica was finding it difficult to keep up with me.

At one point the son told his parents it was time to share the same bed again. At this, his mother looked horrified, but when her husband roared with laughter, she gave way and joined him, whispering private words in his ear. Smiling broadly, they explained to Monica that since their son's death they had slept in separate beds and that only that morning they had decided to put an end to it. Let me explain, though, that whilst 'dead' loved ones are often around our homes and places of work, for instance, they never intrude upon private occasions. Yet often they will mention everyday events to prove their nearness.

This was a truly successful sitting and as ever, I felt privileged and humbled to have acted as a medium between the two worlds, to part the so-called 'veil' and reunite loved ones. To witness two strained and lifeless people become completely animated and full of laughter was like watching a miracle take place. Even more pleasing was the way that Roberto's father strutted around the dining area of Casa del Albero afterwards, telling his joyous news to anyone and everyone who would listen. Apparently he was saying, 'My boy knew what I did for him and he's happy.'

All mediums would agree that they can never remember every message they have given. Some stick in your mind because they have been so touching or uplifting to the recipient whilst others are just shocking. Keeping this in mind, I will tell you of a message that was given during one of the sessions in Italy. All I have changed are the names. I think that you will see why.

It was the last day of a very busy week. 'Just two more sittings to go,' I said to Monica with a degree of relief. No matter how much mediums enjoy their work, their energy will begin to deplete like that of anyone else who has worked non-stop for an entire week. It becomes more difficult to concentrate and tune in, and even the translators begin to flag in the latter stages. Their minds tire of thinking in two different languages and sometimes there are difficulties in translating certain phrases or terms without losing the essence of the comm unication.

Monica and I were both sitting in our room waiting for the next sitter, whom we thought was to be a lady, when in walked a tall good-looking man in his early thirties. Dressed immaculately in designer trousers and open-necked shirt, he never looked in my direction at all, but instead addressed my translator in Italian, then proceeded to sit down.

Monica explained to me that the sitting was booked in someone else's name, but that this gentleman had decided to come along instead. The reason he had spoken to Monica was twofold. One was that he claimed he couldn't speak English. The other was that mediums are never allowed to see the names or any other details of a sitter before or after a sitting.

Once these preliminaries had all been attended to, we got underway. The first person to communicate was a female spirit, who told me her name was Franca. She said she was the man's aunt and added that she had died naturally.

When this information was translated, the sitter responded by asking whether I was quite certain about what she had said. 'Yes, she assures me she died naturally,' I replied. I continued by saying that she had lived and died in Switzerland, and the sitter accepted this. More information came through about her life and the sitter understood all of it. But something in my gut told me I was not answering the questions he had come with.

Then a second communicator came through, saying he was the man's father. Monica began to translate. When I gave the name of Mario Bonetti, both my translator's and the man's mouths fell open at the same time.

No one spoke except for me. 'He tells me,' I said, 'that you have taken over the family business and have done well so far, but this new contract is not worth bothering about.'

Mario then went on to describe a beautiful mountaintop village in Sicily, where he had lived for most of his life, as well as giving more instructions to his son on certain business deals for the future. Just before the translation began, I instructed Monica not to bother as I was told from the Other Side that the sitter had been misleading us and spoke perfect English.

The sitting ended with me asking the man if he had any further questions. He wanted to know if I had access to information on people who came for sittings. At this, Monica jumped in and defended all the mediums who work at the centre. She pointed out that this man had only to look at the name in which he had booked – that of a woman – which had no other information accompanying it.

I might have an awareness of people in the spirit world, but there are times when I really can't see the wood for the trees in an earthly sense! Only after the chat at the end of the sitting did I have any understanding of whom I was speaking to – especially when he asked me if his father meant that there was no need to carry out the contract on the people who were close to his Aunt Franca when she died. Try to imagine the horror I felt when I realized that the father was not describing a family business as such and that the contracts involved doing away with people! Still, all's well that ends well and our young businessman went away with a whole new intention – I hope.

Going home on the plane, Sue and I shared some stories of the week and when I told her of this particular sitting she just laughed, saying, 'Really! Nothing will ever shock me about this place. I've heard it all before.' Apparently she had encountered many such people over the years working in Italy. Mediums really do come across many strange situations on their travels and even though some are really weird, there are still more that turn out to be *magnifico*.

People often say to me, 'Gordon, it must be so exciting travelling around the world.' It is – up to a point. What they forget are the delays at airports, living out of a suitcase and the hours spent at 30,000 feet as a plane drones on. Believe me, there's nothing very exotic about being told that your plane will be delayed for yet another hour or waiting at the carousel for what seems like ages for luggage to emerge, then queuing at customs or passport control for an eternity.

Yet at the end of the day, I literally thank God for my mediumship. Don't get me wrong – I really am just an average, normal guy, but one with a psychic gift. I regard my mediumship as both sacred and spiritual, something not to be used for personal gain, but solely to help others. My role is not to convert anyone, but to say, 'This is what I believe. Test the evidence and reach your own conclusion.'

Personally, I have an unshakeable belief in survival after death and in the spirit world. To me, it's as real and tangible as this one. No one can take that away from me, no matter what they say or do, no matter how harsh or hurtful any criticism that might be levelled at me.

I cannot give my certainty that we are immortal beings temporarily on Earth to anyone. But if nothing else, what I can offer is the hope of survival after death. Whilst this forms a cornerstone of all the world's religions, Spiritualism is the only one to offer *evidence* that we retain our memories, personalities, intelligence and individuality after we pass on.

The spirit world really is one of endless possibilities – a place where the aged regain their youth, the sick and infirm, whether in mind or body, are whole once again, where reunion occurs with all who are dear to us. Love is at the very core of this. It is because of links of love that so-called 'dead' family and friends return to those left on Earth. Love is a golden guiding force, a magical, magnetic link between here and Hereafter.

I'm not a preacher. Far from it! I rarely – if ever – quote from the Bible, yet the three simple words 'Love one another' neatly sum up just part of my personal philosophy of life and death. If we can

When you travel and work as a medium, you don't normally get a chance to see much of the places you visit. That's why I felt a little apprehensive when I was asked to work as far away as Australia. I didn't like the thought of more travel in my already busy schedule, and to a place that was not just a few short hours away but over 20! And that was just the initial journey. Then, while I was in Australia, I had to travel between three state capitals. And the size of the place! Well, you can imagine I was hesitant.

Still, as always, I tuned in mentally to the spirit world and sent the idea out to those who guide me. Instantly, I got a strong feeling – one that surprised me. I felt overwhelmingly excited! I immediately knew that those in the spirit world who guide my work were giving me the go ahead – and once I'd agreed to do it, I started to look forward to my journey to the other side of the world more and more.

The day came to fly out. It was August 2003. I was to arrive in Sydney, where I would stay for five days. The first four days I could rest, then I had to get up on stage and do my first demonstration. After that I would fly to Melbourne, where I would do another demonstration before I flew back to Sydney to do publicity – press interviews, book signings and so on. There was to be more of the same in Brisbane. Though the schedule seemed demanding, whenever my mind crossed over to the spirit world, I was reminded of the strong positive energy that my helpers would be sending me while I was on the tour. All I had to do was trust and they would do the rest.

I felt a rush of excitement when the plane made its approach to Sydney Airport and I saw the entire city, with the world-renowned Harbour Bridge and Opera House, lit up beneath me. It was a magical sight. I felt like a child arriving at my first holiday resort and I couldn't wait to go out and explore the beautiful new world.

I was greeted by Leon Nacson, my Australian host and the organizer of the Intuitive Messengers tour that I was to be part of. Within minutes I felt comfortable with him and we arrived at the exquisite Sheraton Hotel at Hyde Park in no time.

The next few days had been designated as relaxation time for me and the other three people I would be working with on the tour, but instead I decided to see as much of the place as I could. I felt constant awe at just how marvellous everything was. I also felt very much at home – a home painted with joy.

On the morning of our first mediumship demonstration, I was nervous. I was suddenly reminded that I was here to work and even though I've done what I was about to do thousands of times, every new occasion feels like the first the moment before you step out there. The Sydney venue was packed, with some 2,000 people eagerly waiting to hear if their loved ones would bring through a message of love.

As I stepped on stage – in my kilt – I remember seeing a sea of smiling faces and hearing loud applause. I mentally asked the spirit world to help me. As soon as the room had quietened and I had introduced myself, I heard my first Australian accent from the Other Side. Mr John Richardson had come through. He was asking for his daughter, who was sitting right at the back of the hall. I knew that I was tuned in and that things would be fine. After that initial message, they came thick and fast, and I can't remember anything else except the applause at the end.

After the first demonstration, I felt more relaxed about the work and began to look forward to the press interviews. Most were similar to the many I had experienced back in the UK and elsewhere in the world, but one stands out in my mind: a morning radio show hosted by two young men, Merrick and Rosso. Their show is satirical and witty. They're known to tease guests and can be quite flippant and dismissive about certain subjects. They also have a reputation for breaking up interviews after a few minutes and expelling guests from their show! So I had to be prepared!

The interview started and I survived the first five minutes unscathed. After that, Merrick and Rosso seemed to take interest in my work and before I knew it half an hour had passed. The show went something like this – with a bit of nip and tuck!

MR: What's your definition of a psychic?

GS: Well, I'm a medium, which is slightly different. I talk to people who have died. Where psychics will do a reading about your life, the person I'm speaking to has actually passed away and is related to the sitter.

MR: But when these spirits – if I can call them spirits – are sort of hanging around, can you ask them questions, Gordon, serious questions, like 'What is the meaning of life?' and 'Where do people go when they die?'

GS: I usually ask that when I'm a bit drunk, but I never really get the answers! Who really wants to know the meaning of life? I mean, what's the point of living if you know all this stuff?

MR: But have you ever asked a spirit, 'Where does everybody go when they die?'

GS: We're not people when we die, we're spirits. We're consciousness, that's the way I'd look at it. A lot of people assume that the spirit world is like Earth, although with better back-lighting because everybody's bright and shiny. But we're not people anymore, we're consciousness without the physical body, that's all, and it functions differently. That's what happens to the best of my knowledge, but I'm just the medium, I'm just the messenger, so I don't really have all the answers to that stuff. I only know what people tell me, or what spirit people tell me when they come through. But that may differ from person to person.

MR: Are there such things as bad spirits, or evil spirits?

GS: I don't think so, no. I'm not even sure there are bad people. I think people's actions can be good or bad, but people in general are pretty OK. When you are no longer in a physical world, what's the point of lust, jealousy, all those things that make people bad, or make their actions bad? I don't mean that every-body becomes angelic when they die. Their personality still has to come through so they can be recognized. But what's the point of performing a bad action when you're in spirit form?

MR: You don't charge for your services. Why is that?

GS: I've just never done it. I don't know, I've just never felt the need to take money from people. It's very difficult. I see a lot of people who have lost children, and to try and put a price on somebody's grief, on their bereavement, is pretty sore. I just don't work that way.

MR: So what's your opinion of people who do?

GS: I don't have an opinion on people who do that. People can make money, that's up to them. I just don't. When I say I don't make money, of course I make money in my life. I'm a barber, I've got my own business, that's the way I ground myself. That's what I do. But not charging also means that I can be honest with people. I mean, many times people come to me and I just don't get anything and I can say that to them because there is no charge at the end of it. I don't have to sit there and make something up. It cancels out the argument of a lot of the sceptics as well, because what's my motive for doing this? It's certainly not to do with money.

MR: How do you feel when people don't believe?

GS: I've got nothing to prove, I'm not on

trial, so it doesn't bother me if people don't believe. Maybe they're not ready to. I mean, not everybody should consult mediums. You know, they really shouldn't.

Listener 1: My father died in the middle of July and I just want to know, is he OK and is he with me?

GS: When we have a loss like that, the first thing we want to know is if that person is OK. But I can assure you that he's obviously in a much better state than you are at the moment. He no longer has the pains or illnesses that his body had. But I don't have a system where somebody in the spirit world goes through files for me and says, 'Right, I've got your father here.' You have to resonate with the person first of all, so I honestly can't tell you if he is with you. But if you loved the guy, then he's going to be around you.

Listener 2: My dad's been dead for a long time now, since I was about seven years old, and my grandfather passed away about three years ago. I've been told I've got psychic ability and I can feel that they're trying to say something to me, but I don't know what it is.

GS: Any psychic – and it differs slightly from a medium – any psychic has to learn to understand their own feelings before they try and understand the feelings of somebody they can't see. So it's about getting in touch with yourself first. That's what all mediums and psychics have to do. You have to know how you feel, how you actually resonate in this world before you start talking to 'dead' people. And you have to learn that the spirit world doesn't talk to you as audibly as I'm speaking to you now. They can, but more often than not it's a feeling thing.

Listener 2: Would it be best to go to someone to talk about it?

GS: Yeah, well, there's probably a Spiritualist church here [in Sydney] where you can actually go along and become part of a development group. And the thing to remember is, don't just dive into this stuff. I mean, people will tell you, 'Oh yeah, you're going to be a medium.' But if somebody told me I was going to be a stripper, I wouldn't just take my clothes off.

MR: So there's a school you can go to where you can actually hone your skills?

GS: Yeah, back home there are a lot of places and one of the first things I say to people is, 'Why do you want to do this?' They've got to have a genuine desire to help people.

MR: If people aren't grieving, do they get messages? For instance, I'm in a situation where I know people who have passed on but I'm not grieving about anyone. Is it likely that anyone would want to talk to me?

GS: Well, that can happen. Just supposing, say, that you were starting a new television show tomorrow night and you were concerned about how it was going to turn out, then somebody in the spirit world might come through to let you know that it would be OK.

Listener 3: I'm actually going to see a psychic medium today at lunchtime and I want to connect with my mum. What I can expect and how much information should I give?

GS: None.

Listener 3: Should I just sit there and try not to say anything?

GS: Try not to be over-sceptical, because you're doing yourself no favours, but simply respond with 'yes' and 'no'. Don't say you've lost your mum. Just sit there and the psychic will do whatever they need to do to tune in. If they say, 'Oh, I have a lady here,' don't say, 'Oh, it's my mum,' just say, 'Thank you.' That's it. It's the medium who should be telling you who the lady is. But the best thing you can do on the way there is to send a thought up to your mum, something like 'Can you communicate?' That's all, honestly.

That was the gist of the show. Later that morning when I returned to Leon's office with him, a call came through from the radio station. It was from a woman who works there, Nicole Salisbury, asking whether she could speak to me. Before she could tell me what she wanted, a man in the spirit world told me he wanted to communicate with her. He said he was her father, Graham, and that he'd died the previous Saturday. I'll let Nicole tell the story:

I work for Nova and heard Gordon speak with Merrick and Rosso in the studio. It crossed my mind at the time that it would be interesting to talk to him, but by the time I came into the office, Gordon had left. I went to Merrick and Rosso and said, 'That guy was amazing. It sounded brilliant. So compelling.' Rosso then suggested that I talk to him. I wasn't sure at first. Because it was so sudden and so soon after my father's death, I didn't know if it was the right thing to do or not, but Nic McClure, Merrick and Rosso's producer, who has been in contact with Leon Nacson for quite a few years, gave me his number and strongly suggested that I talk with him. So I rang Leon and Leon put me on to Gordon. I said, 'Hi, I'm Nicole from Nova.' And Gordon said, 'Hi, how can I help you?' I didn't know what to say, but then Gordon said, 'OK. Right.' My dad had come through, and Gordon was surprised that he'd come through so strongly, because it was so soon, and he said that that normally doesn't happen. Gordon basically did all of the talking, I just sat there, blubbered and listened. It was just an incredible experience. I couldn't thank Gordon enough for it because to be able to get that kind of reassurance – that my dad was OK – was a gift.

Nicole's father also wanted to speak to her mother, who lived in Brisbane. When I told Nicole I'd be in Brisbane that coming weekend, she was delighted. It's because of 'coincidences' like these that I have learned to trust more and more in the spirit world – it knows exactly what needs to be done and who needs its help. I'm just here to deliver the message. I had a private sitting with Nicole's mother, Marjory, and here's what she had to say about the message I gave her:

I didn't know Gordon was out here. I didn't even know there was a psychic demonstration on at the Convention Centre, but Leon Nacson rang me and said I had to be there, because Gordon had told Nic that he had to talk to me, so … I went along.

When Gordon did the reading, Graham tried so hard to get across so much information that Gordon found it hard to say everything Graham wanted him to. I knew that would be him!

Also, my Aunt Edna came through. She had actually died the same day as Graham. We were expecting her death because she had lung cancer. She died at seven o'clock in the morning and Graham died at three o'clock that afternoon. He had a massive heart attack. Every artery was blocked. The doctor said he would have been dead before he hit the ground.

It was amazing that my Aunt Edna was standing next to Graham. Gordon said she was standing there as if to say, 'Told you so!' I thought that would be right. My Aunt Edna didn't really like Graham and she always called me by my maiden name. Gordon said that Edna wanted me to know that she didn't fear her death, she wanted to die and that she was happy, she was with her sister with flowers around her, lots of flowers. And I said, 'That'd be right, because she loved her garden.'

Graham wanted me to know how sorry he was and how much he loved children. I thought, I know that. He was forever telling me how sorry he was. But when Edna came through I was surprised. I'd never even thought of her. But I was told she would be my strength. She would watch over me and always be with me.

It never ceases to amaze me how quickly some people can come through from the Other Side and when they do, I always find that they have some sort of unfinished business to attend to.

I also had two messages to deliver to the staff at Hay House. I will let them describe the experience in their own words. The first was for Greg Conan:

Leon mentioned to me that Gordon would probably be able to give me a reading, but he didn't say anything about Gordon actually having a message for me. It wasn't until Gordon started to do the reading that I knew he had a specific message for me because it came through so quickly.

There were two people trying to get in touch with me through Gordon. The first person who came through – and who has been with me my whole life – was my grandfather on my mother's side. He died six weeks before I was born and I was his first grandchild. He told me to do what I'd already decided to do. It was confirmation of what I had in mind. He also told Gordon about a huge change I had been through a couple of years ago. I was told that I didn't need to feel guilty about anything I did then because we all go through our trials and tribulations and no one judges you from the Other Side, which is something that had been on my mind.

The other person who came through was Rene, who was like my second mum. She was always on my back about giving up cigarettes and she used to tell me to take life with both hands and live it, without worrying about what everybody else would think. And she gave that message again through Gordon, so I knew it was her. He was coming through with Jeannie or Jenny or something like that, and I realized it was Rene (pronounced 'Ren-ny'). I miss Rene a lot at the moment because she was there for so many years and she's just passed over. I think about her every time I light up a cigarette and every time I do, I hear her say, 'Put it out!' That was another message too! Gordon said she'd been through a hell of a lot in her life – which she had – and that's she's happy now.

The second message was for Rachelle Charman: *What surprised me was that Gordon didn't have a message from a dearly departed relative, but from my spirit guide. I have never divulged to anyone who he is or that he is communicating with me, yet Gordon was able to access information for me. It was like speaking directly to my soul. I couldn't hold back the tears and emotion. I had an inner knowing of everything Gordon spoke of, but it was so empowering to get this sort of confirmation. I felt it was a validation on the deepest level – and that was what was so profound. It was a truly healing experience.*

As I was leaving, Gordon threw in, 'Oh, by the way, get a passport, because you'll be travelling really soon.' I said, 'It's highly unlikely. I have no plans to travel overseas,' but within a week I was invited to Hawaii to be a part of Doreen Virtue's Angel Therapy Practitioner course – as her guest!

I also had a message for Leon that wasn't from a relative, and I think it came as a bit of a shock. I'll let Leon explain:

Many people accused me of organizing the Intuitive Messengers tour schedule so I just happened to be in Brisbane on the night my team, St George, played Brisbane. Would I do a thing like that? I was just as surprised as everyone else when I found out that my beloved Dragons were playing on the Friday night before Saturday night's seminar. That a minibus big enough to seat 14 people had suddenly arrived at the hotel in time to get to the game was just a coincidence!

The bus zoomed down the highway with everyone dressed in St George jerseys, waving red-and-white flags and singing 'When the Saints Come Marching In', right in the heart of enemy territory. I turned to Gordon and said, 'Sorry, mate, to take you to a game where my team is going to get slaughtered, but at least we'll enjoy a night out.'

'Don't worry. You'll do fine,' Gordon replied.

'Yeah, right,' I said. 'You'll have more chance of seeing the Beatles reunite and

perform on the halfway line than of St George winning.' We had eight players out and Brisbane had 14 representative level players on the field. Also, this was a must-win game for Brisbane if they wanted to get into the tournament finals.

'Don't worry,' Gordon insisted. 'It'll be close – very, very close – but you've nothing to worry about.'

On our way to our seats, we saw one of our star players on his mobile phone and we seized the opportunity to have our photo taken with him. (The photo later ended up on the St George website.) Gordon nudged me and said, 'There's a sign. You've got nothing to worry about.' I thought, Forget about the sign, he should be inside warming up.

The game started and by halftime it didn't look good. It looked as if the floodgates would open any second and we would be at the receiving end of the worst defeat in history. But inch by inch, yard by yard, point by point, we edged closer and with one minute to go, our team was left with a penalty kick from an impossible position. Our kicker kicks the ball and it sails through the posts. We won by one point with one second to spare!

To this day, I don't know what amazed me more, the win or Gordon's prediction – not only of the outcome but the type of outcome.

I said to Gordon, 'Mate, next year you can help me with my footy tab.'

Of all the people I met on my Australian tour, no one showed me more of the spirit and true grace of the people who live there than rock singer and Aussie icon Jimmy Barnes and his wife Jane. These warm-hearted people reflected what I felt was the true nature of Australia. My visit to their home left me feeling uplifted – it's so good to know that in a world full of materialism and greed, there are still people who are quick to show compassion and kindness. I felt it was a great privilege to spend some time with a man who has shared the stage with some of the great rock and pop legends of my lifetime and who is still so down to earth and honest ... but then he was born in Glasgow!

Jimmy and I had a special connection – and there's a special story associated with it. I usually wear an ornament of a Buddha around my neck, but on the day I visited Jimmy and Jane I didn't put it on. It was a special surprise, then, when Jimmy gave me the Buddha he usually wears around his neck. During World War II, Jane's grandfather had found a Buddha encased in plaster in the basement of one of the homes he owned. It was brought up with a crane and on the way up was dropped. A chink of the plaster came off and underneath was a gold Buddha. No, before you ask, it wasn't that Buddha that dangled from my neck! Jane's grandfather gave that Buddha to the Temple of the Golden Buddha in Bangkok. But when Jane visits her family in Thailand, she often buys Buddha ornaments from the temple for family and friends, and the Buddha Jimmy gave me was one Jane had bought him a couple of years ago. What a gift!

A similar experience also happened to Jane herself on the same day. She often wears an ornament of the goddess Tara around her neck, though on the day that I visited she hadn't put it on. My gift to her was a postcard of Green Tara. My Tibetan Buddhist friend, Dronma, the psychic artist, had painted the original picture – with the single hair of a paintbrush.

It was nearly time for me to return home, but not before one final blessing. I was sitting with my colleague Doreen Virtue, whom I'd shared the Intuitive Messengers bill with, along with John Holland and Sonia Choquette. She asked me if I'd been aware that I was holding my shoulder and if I was in any pain. I explained that it was an injury that had resulted from many years of hairdressing and that I'd just got used to it.

As well as being a great medium, Doreen also has wonderful healing abilities, as does her husband, Steven Farmer. Both Doreen and Steven asked if they could work on my shoulder to see if it might ease some of the pain. I agreed and within minutes I felt the strain in my neck and shoulder – which I had been carrying throughout the trip – disappear. Such healing ability never ceases to amaze me, even though I have witnessed it many times before.

The spirit world had promised me an exciting trip, and as always they'd been right. As the plane lifted off the runway and turned to go north, I looked down at Sydney Harbour and smiled. I thanked the spirit world for the many wonderful times I had experienced on my journey and I reminded myself of the true rewards that I have received in my life and for my work as a medium.

I have been blessed by God and through my work He has blessed many others. Proving the reality of survival after death to others has become my life's work and I am dedicated to it. I can't say I'll prove it to the entire world. But I'll have fun trying.

ALSO AVAILABLE BY
GORDON SMITH

THE UNBELIEVABLE TRUTH

In this, Gordon's second book, he answers the questions he is most often asked by the people he meets. Gordon explains how the world of Spirit works and how Spirit communicates; he covers ghosts, hauntings, out of body experiences and much more. Ideal for anyone searching for more information on this huge subject area and a perfect accompaniment to *Through My Eyes* and *Spirit Messenger*.

Don't forget you can find out more about Gordon Smith, his life, his work and his upcoming personal appearances by visiting his official website: www.psychicbarber.com

THROUGH MY EYES

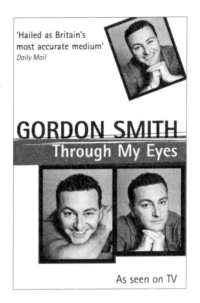

Thousands of people have come to Gordon seeking healing. From them he has gained a profound insight into the true nature of grief and our relationship with the Spirit world. In this his third book, join Gordon as he describes the true nature of grief, how it affects us and our loved ones who have crossed over. An uplifting and insightful book guaranteed to bring peace of mind to anyone who has been touched by loss.

Don't forget you can find out more about Gordon Smith, his life, his work and his upcoming personal appearances by visiting his official website: www.psychicbarber.com

We hope you enjoyed this Hay House book.
If you would like to receive a free catalogue
featuring additional Hay House books and
products, or if you would like information about
the Hay Foundation, please contact:

Hay House UK, Ltd
Unit B, 292 Kensal Road
London W10 5BE
• *Phone:* 020-8962-1230 • *Fax:* 020-8962-1239
• www.hayhouse.co.uk

***

Published and distributed in Australia by:
Hay House Australia, Ltd
18/36 Ralph St., Alexandria NSW 2015
• *Phone:* 612-9669-4299 • *Fax:* 612-9669-4144
• *E-mail:* info@hayhouse.com.au

Published and distributed in the United States by:
Hay House, Inc, P.O. Box 5100, Carlsbad, CA 92018-5100
• *Phone:* (760) 431-7695 or (800) 654-5126
• *Fax:* (760) 431-6948 or (800) 650-5115
• www.hayhouse.com

Distributed in Canada by:
Raincoast, 9050 Shaughnessy St, Vancouver, B.C. V6P 6E5
• *Phone:* (604) 323-7100 • *Fax:* (604) 323-2600

***